Legal Aspects of Impeachment

U.S. Department of Justice

Introduction by Thomas Fensch

Legal Aspects of Impeachment

U.S. Department of Justice

Introduction by Thomas Fensch

ISBN 978-1-7337852-8-0 (softcover)
ISBN 978-1-7337852-9-7 (ebook)

New Century Books
8821 Rockdale Road
N. Chesterfield, VA 23236-2150

newcentbks@gmail.com

Cover image courtesy of Pixabay

Contents

Introduction

by Thomas Fensch

"Nothing is more wonderful than the art of being free,
but nothing is harder to learn how to use than freedom."

—Alexis De Tocqueville, *Democracy in America*
circa 1835-1840.

"The public has grasped that the Constitution demands
wrongdoing of a very high order to justify impeachment."

—Laurence H. Tribe, *To End a Presidency:
The Power of Impeachment,* 2018.[1]

"Impeachment should occur when a president's prior misdeeds are so
awful in their own right, and so disturbing a signal of future conduct,
that allowing the president to remain in office poses a clear
danger of great harm to the constitutional order."

—Tribe, *To End a Presidency.*

Impeachment is the most remote and least visited landscape in American political life. In fact, throughout the life of our republic, it has been visited previously only three times: the presidencies of Andrew Johnson, Richard Nixon and Bill Clinton. And perhaps a fourth, — as this is written, June, 2019 — the administration of Donald Trump.

1   Tribe, Laurence, *To End a Presidency: The Power of Impeachment.* New York: Basic Books, 2018.

The impeachment of Andrew Johnson began Feb. 24, 1868, with 11 articles of impeachment. By May of that year, Congress failed to convict him of any of the 11 charges.

On July 29 and 30, 1974, Richard Nixon was charged with three counts: obstruction of justice; abuse of power and contempt of Congress. Two other counts were debated but not approved.

Subsequently, secret recording tapes made in the Oval Office were released and one, the "Smoking Gun" tape, proving his participation in the Watergate cover-up sealed his fate; support in Congress evaporated and Nixon resigned Aug. 9. 1974, just prior to a certain conviction in the Senate. He has been the only President to resign while in office. (He spent the rest of his days working to rehabilitate his reputation.)

During the same time-frame — approximately August, 1974 — the Department of Justice deemed it necessary to establish guidelines for impeachment, thus this document. Impeachment is, as the Justice Department recognized — in the title of a biography of Mark Twain by Ron Powers — *dangerous water*.[2]

Robert G. Dixon Jr., Assistant Attorney General in the Office of Legal Counsel, wrote: "In a broad sense the impeachment material being released consists of attorney working papers of a sort normally not disclosed. In this instance, however, because of the interest surrounding the subject, the extraordinary nature of our present circumstances, and the historically informative nature of this study, a broad sharing of it is deemed by the Department of Justice to be in the public interest."

---

2   Powers, Ron, *Dangerous Water: A Biography of the Boy who Became Mark Twain*. New York: Basic Books, 1999.

The "extraordinary nature of our present circumstances." Dangerous water indeed. The days of Nixon's impeachment.[3]

In fact, as revealed in this study, there is no — and apparently never has been — any "black type," pure definition of "high crimes and misdemeanors." *This ultimate term could be defined by any Congress at any time with its own terminology and with its own rationale.*

Although written during Nixon's impeachment times, this document is essentially a historical study, designed as resource material. The word academic is used in this reference. Nixon is mentioned, although only briefly. The document does not analyze any particular factual allegations, reach ultimate conclusions or propose solutions.

The Department of Justice completed this analysis to stimulate discussion and indicate the complex nature of this most remote, least-visited landscape of our democracy.

Voting citizens, politicians at every level, students, academics and others are urged to read this, the only document of its kind.

Thomas Fensch is the author of 37 previous books of nonfiction. They include: *The Kennedy-Khrushchev Letters*, 2001; *Foreshadowing Trump: Trump characters, ethics, morality and Fascism in classic literature*, 2018 and *Orwell in America*, 2019. He has a doctorate from Syracuse University and lives outside Richmond, Virginia.

---

3   Bill Clinton was impeached 24 years later Dec. 1998, thus was not included in this study.

Department of Justice

LEGAL ASPECTS OF IMPEACHMENT: AN OVERVIEW

Office of Legal Counsel
Department of Justice
February 1974

TABLE OF CONTENTS

Preface

This overview memorandum summarizes the work of the
staff of the Office of Legal Counsel in regard to impeachment. The views expressed should not be regarded as
official positions of the Department of Justice.

The major topics in this memorandum are dealt with
more fully in four appendices. Although the research has been
extensive, this material does not purport to be an exhaustive
survey.

Work on the subject began in October and was expanded
considerably in December as time and the pressure of other
work permitted. The study is an independent, objective,
and essentially historical survey of the field, designed to
serve as resource material in the academic sense. It does
not analyze any particular factual allegations, reach ultimate
conclusions, or propose solutions. The material may serve to
illuminate discussion and indicate the complexity of
impeachment.

Appendices I and II dealing with historical material on
the concept of impeachable offenses, drawn from the debates
in the Constitutional Convention, other materials contemporary
to that period, and instances of impeachment action in the past,

were completed and released on February 21, 1974. We now release an overview statement, and Appendices III and IV setting forth respectively a collation of executive privilege statements where impeachment also was mentioned, and a collation of comment on the question of judicial review of an impeachment conviction.

In a broad sense the impeachment material being released consists of attorney working papers of a sort normally not disclosed. In this instance, however, because of the interest surrounding the subject, the extraordinary nature of our present circumstances, and the historically-informative nature of this study, a broad sharing of it is deemed by the Department of Justice to be in the public interest.

Robert G. Dixon, Jr.
Assistant Attorney General
Office of Legal Counsel

B. Provisions of the Constitution

Impeachment is dealt with or referred to in six provisions of the Constitution, as follows:

1. Impeachment power of House of Representatives

Article I, section 2, clause 5 provides in part that: "The House of Representatives . . . shall have the sole power of impeachment."

2. Senate power to try impeachments

Article I, section 3, clause 6 is as follows:

The Senate shall have the sole power to try all impeachments. When sitting for that purpose, they shall be on oath or affirmation. When the President of the United States is tried, the Chief Justice shall preside: And no person shall be convicted without the concurrence of two thirds of the members present.

3. Sanctions

Article I, section 3, clause 7 provides as follows:

Judgment in cases of impeachment shall not extend further than to removal from office, and disqualification to hold and enjoy any office of honor, trust or profit under the United States: but the party convicted shall nevertheless be liable and subject to indictment, trial, judgment and punishment, according to law.

4. Inapplicability of pardon power

Article II, section 2, clause 1 states that "The President . . . shall have power to grant reprieves and pardons for offenses against the United States, except in cases of impeachment."

5. Grounds for impeachment

Article II, section 4 is as follows:

> The President, Vice President and all civil officers of the United States, shall be removed from office on impeachment for, and conviction of, treason, bribery, or other high crimes and misdemeanors.

6. Inapplicability of right to jury trial

Article III, section 2, clause 3 states in part that: "The trial of all crimes, except in cases of impeachment shall be by jury; . . . ."[1]

The history of the provisions of the Constitution which relate to impeachment is discussed below in part C.

1/ The right to trial by jury is also dealt with in the Sixth Amendment which refers to "all criminal prosecutions," but does not mention the matter of impeachment.

C. Grounds for Impeachment

The grounds for impeachment set forth in Article II, section 4 of the Constitution are "treason, bribery, or other high crimes and misdemeanors." The meanings of "treason"[2]/ and "bribery"[3]/ are relatively clear. On the other hand, the meaning of "high crime and misdemeanor," though the subject of considerable debate in impeachment proceedings and elsewhere, remains uncertain.

The fundamental issue is whether a "high crime or misdemeanor" must be a criminal offense. The view that criminal conduct is required has been asserted by, among others, counsel for Justice Chase in 1804, for Andrew Johnson in 1868 and for William O. Douglas in 1970. The primary basis for this view is the language of the Constitution. "Crime," "misdemeanor" and "conviction" are

---

2/ See Article III, section 3 of the Constitution; 18 U.S.C. 2381.

3/ See 18 U.S.C. 201.

terms used in criminal law.$^{4/}$ Most other references to
impeachment in the Constitution are in contexts which
suggest criminal proceedings. E.g., Art. I, § 3, cl. 7
(liability to "indictment . . ."), Art II, § 2, cl. 1
(pardon of "offenses"). One can contend that the

_____

4/ It should be noted that Raoul Berger asserts that
"high crimes and misdemeanors" is a term of art, derived
from British practice in impeachment cases and that
"high misdemeanor" was not a term of criminal law when
the Constitution was adopted. However, the distinction
is clouded because the British could and did impose
criminal penalties in impeachment.

Ordinary rules of construction may yield opposing
conclusions. On the one hand, it may be argued that,
if it had been intended to limit the grounds to crimes,
use of the term "misdemeanors" in the phrase "high
crimes and misdemeanors" would not have been necessary.
On the other hand, the phrase "treason, bribery, or
other high crimes and misdemeanors" suggests that what
follows "other" is criminal, just as treason and bribery
are crimes.

language of the Constitution is sufficiently clear that resort to other sources is unnecessary. [5]

The position that violation of criminal law is not a prerequisite for impeachment rests upon the view that the underlying purpose of the impeachment process is not to punish the individual, but is to protect the public against gross abuse of power. Thus, while not all crimes would rise to the level of impeachable offense, certain types of non-criminal conduct, under this view, could warrant removal from office.

A few opinions of the Supreme Court contain dictum regarding impeachment, [6] but there is no actual court

---

[5] Assuming that criminal conduct is required, further issues are what body of criminal law is to be relied upon (British common law, the federal code, etc.) and what standard is to be used in distinguishing "high crimes" or "high misdemeanors" from other offenses.

[6] Contrast Ex parte Grossman, 267 U.S. 87, 121 (1925) (suggestion that Presidential abuse of the pardon power might warrant impeachment) and Kilbourn v. Thompson, 103 U.S. 168, 193 (1880) (suggestion that "criminality" is a prerequisite for impeachment).

decision with respect to grounds for impeachment under
the United States Constitution. $\underline{7/}$ Accordingly, available sources include materials on the history of the
Constitution, congressional precedents in impeachment
cases, and scholarly works.

1. History of the Constitutional Provisions.

   a.   The Constitutional Convention

   (May 25 to September 17, 1787)

The subject of impeachment of the chief executive
was raised at an early point during the Convention, but
the phrase "high crimes and misdemeanors" was not decided
upon until September 8, near the end of the Convention.

At different times during the Convention, various
other formulations of the grounds for impeachment were
considered, including "mal-practice or neglect of duty;"
"treason, bribery or corruption;" and "treason or
bribery." Thus, in considering statements made during

_____

7/   There are a number of state court impeachment cases,
but these relate to state constitutions and thus are of
limited relevance.

the Convention, it is important to bear in mind the precise language being debated. Also pertinent is the closely related issue of the manner in which the chief executive was to be chosen. This matter received more attention than did the question of impeachment. Some delegates favored a strong legislature, the functions of which would include selecting the chief executive. Others were concerned about undue concentration of power in the legislature. Similar views were expressed in regard to impeachment. For example, Pinckney of South Carolina was opposed to impeachment on the ground that it was unnecessary and would give Congress undue control over the executive. Others (e.g., Madison) favored in-clusion of a provision on impeachment as a safeguard against abuse of power on the part of the President.

Available records regarding the Constitutional Convention [8/] provide no clear answer concerning the meaning of "high crimes and misdemeanors." No discussion of that phrase took place in the context of

---

[8/] See Farrand, The Records of the Federal Convention of 1787 (1937).

impeachment. The only specific discussion of the term

"high misdemeanor" was in debate over extradition pro-

visions. In regard to extradition, on August 28, "high

misdemeanors" was rejected in favor of "other crimes,"

because the former had a "technical meaning" which was

considered to be too limited. A short time later,

"high crimes and misdemeanors" was substituted for "mal-

administration" as a justification for impeachment because

the latter term was regarded as being too vague. $\underline{9}$/

Presumably, the Framers intended "high crimes and mis-

demeanors" to have a rather limited technical meaning.

On the basis of the Convention notes, the fol-

lowing observations may be warranted:

(1) The term "high crimes and misdemeanors"   neanors

meant something narrower than "maladministration." The

notion that a President could be removed at the pleasure

of the Senate was rejected.

$\underline{9}$/ Many of the state constitutions which were in effect
in 1787 included "maladministration" as a ground for
impeachment.

(2) Although there was a passing reference at the Convention to the impeachment of Warren Hastings of the British East India Company, which was then pending in England, there was no clear intent to adopt wholesale English practice and precedent on impeachment. Clearly, many aspects of British practice (e.g., imposition of criminal punishment) were rejectd.

(3) Appropriate weight must be given to the discussions at the Convention which suggested that impeachment would be available for non-criminal offenses. Still, most such discussions took place some six weeks before the adoption of the term "high crimes and misdemeanors." At that time, the phrase before the Convention was "malpractice or neglect of duty," clearly a much broader definition than the final text.

It might be said, of course, that those who six weeks before had advocated a broader clause would have objected if they thought that the language finally adopted did not meet their intentions. However, another possible inference is that, as the end of the Convention neared, such persons were more ready to compromise.

   b.   The Federalist

   In Federalist No. 65, Alexander Hamilton
discussed impeachment and gave the reasons for the
Senate's being chosen as the forum for trying impeachments.   Indirectly he cast light on the nature of what
was considered impeachable:

> The subjects of its jurisdiction are those
> offenses which proceed from the misconduct of
> public men, or, in other words, from the abuse
> or violation of some public trust. They are of
> a nature which may with peculiar propriety be
> denominated POLITICAL as they relate chiefly to
> injuries done immediately to the society itself.
> (The Federalist, The Central Law Journal Co.,
> St. Louis, 1914, vol. 2, p. 17).

Hamilton also noted that an impeachment case "can never
be tied down by such strict rules . . . in the delineation of the offense by the prosecutors, or in the construction of it by the judges, as in common cases serve
to limit the discretion of the courts in favor of
personal security." Id. at 19. He spoke of "The awful
discretion which a court of impeachments must necessarily have . . ." as a reason for not giving the power
to try impeachments to the Supreme Court. Ibid.

   Thus, Hamilton's analysis cuts against the
argument that "high crimes and misdemeanors" should be
limited to criminal offenses.

10/ There were delegates who supported even narrower
grounds, such as "treason or bribery" and some who thought
that an impeachment provision was not necessary at all.

c. <u>State ratification conventions</u>

The state ratification debates were, with the exception of Virginia, New York, and North Carolina, badly or very incompletely reported. In three states -- Delaware, New Jersey, and Georgia -- the convention proceedings were not reported at all. The limited information available with regard to the state conventions makes it difficult to draw any firm conclusions, on the basis of the·debate at those conventions, regarding the meaning of the Constitution.

One view which was expressed (e.g., by Iredell of North Carolina) was that impeachable offenses must be "great" ones. <u>11</u>/

There were other statements showing a variety of ideas as to the meaning of impeachable offenses. Some examples are: "abuse of trust" (Bowdoin, Massachusetts); acting "from some corrupt motive" (Iredell, North Carolina); commission of a high crime punishable

---

<u>11</u>/ 4 Elliott, <u>The Debates in the several State Conventions on the adoption of the Federal Constitution</u> (1836), p. 113.

at common law (Nicholas, Virginia); the President's being connected with a person in a suspicious manner and sheltering the person, or the President's summoning only a few states to consider a treaty (Madison, Virginia).

Many of these remarks at the ratification conventions describe the impeachment power in terms which include criminal conduct, but which do not necessarily require it. This would be true of such words as "abuse of trust." Certainly, a number of delegates indicated that impeachment could be brought for disregard of the accepted processes of government even though no crime had been committed. An example is Madison's strange hypothetical concerning summoning only a few states in order to secure approval for a treaty.

The records which are available concerning the state ratification debates seem to show more focus on impeachment procedure, than on the precise content of impeachable offense.

2. The First Congress

Statements made at the First Congress are often cited as being authoritative as to the meaning of the Constitution. Pertinent to the matter of impeachment was a debate regarding the power of the President to remove executive officers.

Madison, who argued for the President's right to remove officers by himself, stated the following (1 Annals of Congress 372-373):

> I think it absolutely necessary that the President should have the power of removing from office; it will make him, in a peculiar manner, responsible for their conduct, and subject him to impeachment himself, if he suffers them to perpetuate with impunity high crimes or misdemeanors against the United States, or neglects to superintend their conduct, so as to check their excesses. * * *

Madison also said, concerning the advisability of empowering the President to remove executive officers (1 Annals of Congress 498):

> The danger, then, consists merely in this: the President can displace from office a man whose merits require that he should be continued in it. What will be the motives which the President can feel for such abuse of his power and the restraints that operate to prevent it. In the first place, he will be impeachable by this House before the Senate for such an act of mal-administration; for I contend that the wanton removal of meritorious officers would subject him to impeachment and removal from his own high trust. * * *

The latter quoted statement does not appear to be consistent with what Madison's own notes show that he had said at the Constitutional Convention. He objected at the Convention to impeachment for "maladministration."

3. Americam impeachment precedents

   a. General

   According to the <u>Congressional Quarterly</u>
<u>Guide</u> to the Congress of the United States,[12] impeach-
ment proceedings have been initiated in the House of
Representatives some fifty times since 1789. Only
twelve of these cases reached the Senate.

   Two of the twelve cases involved officials of
the executive branch, President Andrew Johnson (1868)
and Secretary of War William Belknap (1876). President
Johnson was acquitted when the Senate failed, by one
vote, to produce the requisite two-thirds majority for
conviction. Belknap was also acquitted, a major reason
being the fact that he had resigned his office several
months before the Senate trial.

   Senate proceedings against the only Senator to
be impeached, William Blount, were dismissed in 1799 for
lack of jurisdiction; Blount had been expelled by the
Senate in 1797.

_____

12/ Reprinted in part in Impeachment, House Committee
Print, House Judiciary Committee, 93rd Cong., 1st Sess.
(1973), p. 705.

The other nine impeachment cases which reached the Senate involved federal judges.[13] Of these, four were convicted: John Pickering (1804), West H. Humphreys (1862), Robert W. Archbald (1913), and Halsted L. Ritter (1936).

The cases of the twelve federal officers who were impeached by the House of Representatives are obviously pertinent in determining the meaning and scope of "high crimes and misdemeanors." Nonetheless, congressional precedents are quite different from court decisions and, particularly in regard to impeachment of an executive official, there are limits on the relevancy and utility of the congressional precedents.

One complicating fact is that most of the impeachments involved judges. The Constitution provides that federal judges "shall hold their offices during

---

[13] Among the impeachment attempts which failed in the House of Representatives were the following: President Tyler (1843), Vice President Colfax (1873), Attorney General Daugherty (1923), Secretary of the Treasury Mellon (1932), and President Hoover (1932, 1933). The most recent impeachment attempt occurred in 1970 and related to Justice William O. Douglas.

good behavior." Art. III, § 1. "Good behavior" is not specified among the grounds for impeachment set out in Article II, section 4. While the notion that judges can be impeached for misbehavior has been criticized, it is clear from an examination of past impeachments that the proceedings against judges have been influenced by this factor. Thus, matters that might not be considered high crimes and misdemeanors as to non-judicial officers have been deemed as appropriate for inclusion in the articles of impeachment against judges.

In general, it is difficult to determine the weight to be given past acts of Congress in impeachment proceedings. A vote of the House to bring charges can be taken as a judgment that certain acts, if proved, constitute high crimes and misdemeanors. However, as Hamilton pointed out, a "court of impeachments" has an "awful discretion." It would seem that even if grounds were established by the evidence, a Senator is free to vote against conviction because in his view the grounds simply did not warrant removal from office. Thus, failure to muster the necessary two-thirds vote for conviction can be explained in a number of ways and does not

necessarily amount to a holding that the charges were

not high crimes or misdemeanors.

There follows a discussion of the Andrew Johnson

impeachment and brief summaries of the other eleven

impeachments.

b. Impeachment of President Andrew Johnson

As noted above, the impeachment of Andrew Johnson in 1868 was the sole instance in which the House of Representatives impeached a President.

(1) Attempted impeachment (1866-1867)

In 1866, the House agreed to a resolution authorizing the House Judiciary Committee to "inquire into the official conduct of Andrew Johnson" and report whether he had committed a high crime or misdemeanor. [14] The Committee's investigation took more than ten months. The Committee interviewed almost 100 witnesses, including Cabinet officers and the President's personal secretaries. Department and Presidential documents were produced, either voluntarily or in response to Committee requests, and conversations with the President were related. It does not appear that any claim of executive privilege was made.

---

[14] Earlier in 1866, a motion to suspend the rules of the House to permit introduction of a resolution to impeach President Johnson failed to gain the requisite two-thirds vote.

Upon completion of its investigation, the House Judiciary Committee, by a five-to-four majority, recommended impeachment. See H.R. Rep. No. 7, 40th Cong., 1st Sess. (1867). The Committee resolution was voted on by the House and rejected on December 7, 1867.

(2) Impeachment and Senate trial (1868)

The second major effort to impeach Johnson began in January 1868 and was assigned to the Committee on Reconstruction. On February 21, Johnson formally dismissed Secretary of War Edwin M. Stanton, allegedly in violation of the Tenure of Office Act's requirement of Senate consent (which Johnson believed to be unconstitutional). On the following day, the Committee on Reconstruction recommended impeachment of the President. On February 24, the House adopted a resolution impeaching Johnson and appointed a committee to prepare articles of impeachment. Eleven articles were adopted by the House in March.

The first eight articles charged that Stanton's removal was unlawful as an intentional violation of the Tenure of Office Act and the Constitution. Article IX alleged violation of a statute requiring that all military orders pass through the General of the Army. Article X charged that Johnson, by intemperate harangues, had ridiculed Congress. Article XI charged (1) that Johnson had declared tht the 39th Congress represented only part of the states and that accordingly its laws were not binding, and (2) that, pursuant to his declaration, Johnson had attempted to prevent execution of various laws.

After weeks of argument and testimony, Senate votes were taken on Article XI and subsequently on two of the articles relating to the Tenure of Office Act. In each instance, the vote was 35 for and 19 against conviction, one vote short of the two-thirds majority required for conviction. No vote was taken on the remaining articles.

A basic issue was whether "high crime or misdemeanor" meant violation of a criminal law. The President's attorneys asserted the narrow view, i.e., that only criminal conduct could constitute an impeachable offense.

President Johnson did not appear personally at the trial. Apparently no attempt was made by Johnson's counsel to rely upon executive privilege or any related doctrine. The defense attempted to call members of Johnson's Cabinet to testify as to conversations they had had with the President, but the Senate excluded virtually all such evidence.

The atmosphere of the trial was highly partisan. Numerous rulings of Chief Justice Chase, who presided, regarding such matters as introduction of evidence were overruled by the Senate (by a majority vote).

The entire proceeding has been criticized by scholars. For example, in his recent book, Impeachment (1973), p. 295, Raoul Berger refers to it as a "gross abuse of the impeachment process . . . ."

(3) Role of the Attorney General

As noted above, the first major effort to impeach Andrew Johnson involved lengthy (closed) hearings before the House Judiciary Committee. The role of Henry Stanbery, the Attorney General,[15] was not substan-

---

[15] The Department of Justice was not created until 1870. Attorney General Stanbery had a small staff.

tially different from that of other Cabinet members.
The Cabinet had general discussions regarding the House
proceedings, including in particular the question whether
the President might be arrested. Stanbery, as Attorney
General, testified before the House Committee, but it
does not appear that he or any other executive official
represented President Johnson before the House Committee.

The second effort to impeach Andrew Johnson was
completed in a short period of time--one day's consideration in the Committee on Reconstruction and adoption
two days later by the House of an impeachment resolution. There is no evidence that the Attorney General or
any other executive official represented President
Johnson before the Committee on Reconstruction or the
House in this second impeachment attempt.

After adoption of the impeachment resolution on
February 24, 1868, Attorney General Stanbery played an
important role in selecting defense attorneys and in
planning legal strategy. On March 12, 1868, the day before the Senate trial began, Stanbery resigned his

office, and Stanbery and four other private attorneys
represented Johnson in the Senate trial.[16]

Stanbery believed that it would be lawful for
him to retain his office while representing Johnson
before the Senate. The reasons for Stanbery's resignation were twofold: the practical difficulty of
performing both jobs (Attorney General and defense counsel) at the same time; a desire to avoid objections on
the part of members of Senate to his continuing in
office.

_____

[16] There is no evidence of legal assistance provided
by any Government attorneys at the Senate trial.

c. Other impeachments

The eleven impeachments, other than President Johnson's, may be summarized as follows:

Senator William Blount (1798) - charged with violating America's neutrality and federal law by conspiring to transfer to England Spanish property in Florida and Louisiana, conspiring to undermine the confidence of Indian tribes in a federal agent, etc. It does not appear that Blount disputed that the charges amounted to indictable offenses. The Senate dismissed the charges on the ground that Senators are not subject to impeachment.

Judge John Pickering (1804), convicted on four articles - three related to unlawful (but non-criminal) conduct in a suit for condemnation of a ship (e.g., returning the ship to its owner without obtaining a bond as required by law); the fourth article charged that Pickering was intoxicated and used profanity while on the bench. There was evidence that Pickering was insane, but he was convicted nonetheless.

Justice Samuel Chase (1804) - eight articles of impeachment, six based on his actions while presiding at treason and sedition trials; two concerned efforts to exhort grand juries. Chase's counsel, Luther Martin, who had been a delegate at the Constitutional Convention, contended that only an indictable offense was impeachable. The House managers asserted the contrary view in the Senate. Chase was acquitted.

Judge James H. Peck (1830) - charged with wrongfully convicting an attorney of contempt. Peck was acquitted.

Judge West H. Humphreys (1862) - Humphreys, who in 1861 had ceased acting as a federal judge and then act as a Confederate judge, was charged with conduct resembling treason. He did not answer the charges and was convicted.

William W. Belknap (1876) - Belknap resigned as Secretary of War shortly before he was impeached on grounds which amounted to bribery (i.e., receiving payments for appointing a person to be post trader at a fort). He was acquitted.

Judge Charles Swayne (1903) - charged with criminal offenses, including making false claims against the Government. He was acquitted.

Judge Robert W. Archbald of the Commerce Court (1912) - charged with a variety of matters involving improper, but apparently non-criminal, conduct. The "misbehavior" issue was raised. He was found guilty on five articles.

Judge George W. English (1926) - some of the charges bordered on criminal conduct. English resigned before trial and the proceedings were discontinued.

Judge Harold Louderback (1933) - five charges ranging from felonious (false voter registration) to improper conduct. He was acquitted.

Judge Halsted L. Ritter (1936) - seven articles including criminal offenses (tax evasion), and also prejudicing the public's view of the court's fairness. He was acquitted on the specific charges, but convicted on the latter (which reiterated the specific charges).

The foregoing summaries give some indication of the practice in the House, primarily, however, in regard to judges. As noted previously, the issue whether criminal conduct is required is a recurring one, and there is no clear resolution of the question.

4. Scholarly works

The views of commentators have varied. Story maintained that impeachable offenses were political in nature and should not be limited to statutory crimes. Other writers, e.g., Irving Brant in Impeachment, Trials and Errors (1972), have maintained that the only proper grounds for impeachment are indictable offenses.

Raoul Berger maintains that violation of a criminal statute is not a prerequisite for impeachment so long as the offense is a "great" one. A difficulty with Berger's approach is his heavy reliance upon British practice predating the Constitution. Even assuming that his reading of British history is correct (i.e., his view that "high crimes and misdemeanors" is a term of art which dates back to the fourteenth century and which encompasses certain types of non-criminal misbehavior), his conclusion that the Framers intended to follow British practice is open to doubt. For example, the Framers explicitly rejected "maladministration," a concept that had apparently been utilized in England. Moreover, much of the Constitution, including aspects of impeachment, was a reaction against the British system.

5. The foregoing discussion indicates the difficul- ᴸ⁻
ties in attaching a firm meaning to "high crimes and
misdemeanors." Furthermore, the question is decided
first by the House Committee and the 435 members of the
House and then by the Senate. Public statements indicate that various views have been held by the members
of those bodies.

There are persuasive grounds for arguing both
the narrow view that a violation of criminal law is required and the broader view that certain non-criminal
"political offenses" may justify impeachment. While the
narrow view finds support in the language of the Constitution, the terms, particularly "high misdemeanor,"
are not without ambiguity. Post-convention historical
materials, such as the Federalist and the records of the
state ratification conventions, lend support to the view
that impeachment may be based upon certain types of
non-criminal conduct. One conclusion which clearly
emerges is that the "political power" positions advanced
by Mr. Kleindienst in the 1973 Senate hearings on executive privilege (no need for any "facts") or by Mr. Ford

in 1970 regarding the Douglas investigation (any ground adopted by the House) are not supported by pertinent historical sources, although the near-successful impeachment of President Andrew Johnson has been viewed by some as an example of the "political power" view and the Johnson impeachment has been criticized on that ground. There is, however, fairly wide support for an essential premise of the "political power" position, i.e., that judicial review of congressional impeachment action is unavailable.

D. Procedures in the House and the Senate

Procedures followed in the House of Representatives and in the Senate with regard to impeachment are described in annotations to the current edition of Jefferson's Manual of Parliamentary Practice. [17] The annotations summarize pertinent material from Hind's and Cannon's Precedents of the House of Representatives. The Rules of the House of Representatives do not otherwise deal with the matter of impeachment.

The Senate has specific rules of procedure and practice with regard to impeachment trials. [18] There is overlap between the two sets of procedures, due in part to the role of the House (or its managers) in presenting to the Senate the case for impeachment.

1. House impeachment procedures

The House procedures may be summarized as follows

---

[17] See Constitution, Jefferson's Manual and Rules of the House of Representatives, 93rd Congress, House Document No. 384, 92d Cong., 2d Sess. (1973).

[18] See Senate Manual, Senate Document No. 93-1, 93rd Cong., 1st Sess. (1973), pp. 135-146. With one exception, the Senate rules regarding impeachment have been in effect since the 1868 trial of President Andrew Johnson.

(all references are to the 1973 annotated Jefferson's Manual): There are various ways of initiating impeachment proceedings in the House of Representatives, including a resolution introduced by a Member, or facts developed and reported by an investigating committee of the House. (Jefferson's Manual, § 603)

The House may order an immediate investigation or may refrain from doing so until the charges have been examined by a committee. (§ 605) Some early committee investigations were ex parte, but in later practice the committees have favored permitting the accused to explain his case, to present and cross-examine witnesses, and to be represented by counsel. (§ 606)

The investigations are conducted more or less according to the established rules of evidence, but the strict rules of evidence have been relaxed.[19/]

After the investigating committee has reported, the House may vote on the impeachment. If impeachment is voted, the House notifies the Senate by message. (§ 607)

19/ See III Hind's Precedents, §§ 2403 and 2516.

Adoption of articles of impeachment requires a majority in the House.

"Prosecution" of an impeachment is the responsibility of managers who are either elected by the House or, pursuant to a resolution, appointed by the Speaker. (§ 609)

2. Senate trial procedures

Arranging for trial. When the Senate is ready to receive the articles, they are exhibited to the Senate by the House managers. (Jefferson's Manual, § 609; Senate impeachment rules I-II) At the request of the managers, the Senate issues a summons for the appearance of the respondent. (Jefferson's Manual, § 608) This occurs after the Senate has notified the House that the Senate is organized for the trial. (Senate rule VIII)

The accused may appear in person or by attorney to answer the articles. If he does not appear, the trial proceeds as upon a plea of not guilty. (Senate rules VIII and X; Jefferson's Manual, § 611)

Formal pleadings, including the answer of the accused and the replication of the House of Representatives, are filed. (Jefferson's Manual, §§ 612-613) The accused may, for example, demur to the charges on the ground that no "high crime or misdemeanor" is alleged.

When the accused is the President, the Chief Justice presides. (Senate rule IV)

Trial procedures. Before the Senate considers the articles of impeachment, an oath is administered to the members of the Senate by the presiding officer. (Rule III, all references are to the Senate rules on impeachment). The Senate may compel the attendance of witnesses, may enforce obedience to its orders, and may punish contempts in a summary way. (Rule VI)

The presiding officer (i.e., the Chief Justice when the President is the accused) may rule on questions of evidence and other questions, unless a Senator asks that the matter be presented to the Senate for decision (by majority vote). (Rule VII)

Under Rule XI (which was adopted in 1935), the presiding officer, upon order of the Senate, shall appoint a committee of twelve Senators to receive evidence and take testimony at times and places determined by the committee.

Witnesses are sworn and subject to cross-examination. (Rule XVII, rule XXV)

The articles of impeachment are voted on separately. If none of the articles is sustained by a vote of two-thirds of the members present, a judgment of acquittal is entered. If the accused is convicted upon any of the articles by such two-thirds vote, the Senate proceeds to pronounce judgment. (Rule XXIII)

E. Initiation of Impeachment Proceedings with
Respect to the President.

Since May 1973, more than 40 resolutions relating
to impeachment of President Nixon have been introduced
in the House of Representatives. For example, a number
of such resolutions were introduced on October 23, 1973.
The subject matter and amount of detail have varied,
but two basic types of resolution are (1) those which
provide for impeachment of President Nixon for high
crimes and misdemeanors, e.g., H. Res. 625; and those,
e.g., H. Res. 627, which direct the Judiciary Committee
(or another committee) to investigate whether grounds
exist for impeachment of President Nixon. Resolutions
of the former type (impeachment) were referred to the
Judiciary Committee. Resolutions of the latter type
(preliminary investigation by a committee) were referred
to the Rules Committee. See, e.g., 119 Cong. Rec.
H 9356 (daily ed., Oct. 23, 1973).

Subsequently, the Judiciary Committee began to
assemble a staff and to organize an investigation of

the matter of impeachment. [20] On October 30, the Judiciary

Committee met in open session and voted, along party

lines, to authorize the Chairman to issue subpoenas in

connection with "the inquiry into the impeachment of the

President . . . ."

On November 15, 1973, the House debated a resolu-

tion (H. Res. 702), offered by the Committee on House

Administration, to authorize funds for "investigations

and studies to be conducted [by the Judiciary Committee]

pursuant to H. Res. 74." After discussing such matters

as subpoena power and the allocation of funds between

the majority and the minority members, the House author-

ized one million dollars for investigations and studies

by the Judiciary Committee. 119 Cong. Rec. H 10068

(daily ed., Nov. 15, 1973). Neither the resolution author-

izing the funds (H. Res. 702) nor the underlying author-

ization for the activities of the Judiciary Committee

20/ No action has been taken by the Rules Committee with
respect to the resolutions providing for a study by the
Judiciary Committee.

(H. Res. 74)[21/] refers to impeachment.

During the debate on additional funds for the Judiciary Committee, Congressman Wiggins asserted that H. Res. 702 was "technically defective" in that it did not empower the Judiciary Committee to conduct an impeachment investigation. His assertion was based upon the failure of H. Res. 74 and Rule XI to give the Judiciary Committee jurisdiction over impeachment. 119 Cong. Rec. H 10063 (daily ed., Nov. 15, 1973).

On December 20, Chairman Rodino announced that John M. Doar, former, Chairman, New York City School Board and former Assistant Attorney General, Civil Rights Division, would serve as special counsel to the Committee and would direct the inquiry into the existence of grounds for impeachment of President Nixon. On January 7, 1974,

---

21/ H. Res. 74 is set forth at 119 Cong. Rec. H. 1218 (daily ed., Feb. 28, 1973). H. Res. 74 authorizes the Judiciary Committee "to conduct . . . studies and investigations and make inquiries within its jurisdiction as set forth in . . . [Rule XI(13)] of the Rules of the House of Representatives." Rule XI (13) confers jurisdiction on the Judiciary Committee with respect to such matters as judicial proceedings, constitutional amendments and Presidential succession, but it does not refer to impeachment.

it was announced that Albert E. Jenner, Jr. of Chicago
would be the chief minority counsel for the Republican
members of the Judiciary Committee with regard to
impeachment of the President.

On January 7, Chairman Rodino stated that the
Committee hoped to complete its work and report to the
House by late April. The Chairman also announced that
the Committee's subpoena power does not extend to
impeachment and that, after the House reconvenes on
January 21, the Committee would seek express authorization to subpoena persons and documents with regard to
the impeachment inquiry.[22]

22/ H. Res. 74 provides subpoena power for the Judiciary
Committee. However, as noted above, neither H. Res. 74
nor Rule XI (13), whose jurisdictional provisions the
resolution incorporates, mentions impeachment.
    The civil action by the Senate Select Committee to
enforce subpoenas duces tecum against the President was
dismissed by the district court on October 17, 1973.
Senate Select Committee v. Nixon, 366 F. Supp. 5 (D. D.C.).
The basis for the dismissal was lack of jurisdiction. The
Senate Committee appealed and then succeeded in obtaining
a statute which conferred jurisdiction upon the United
States District Court for the District of Columbia over civil
actions brought by the Senate Select Committee to enforce
its subpoenas against the President or other civil officers
(Public Law 93-190). On December 28, the United States Court
of Appeals remanded the suit to the district court for
consideration in light of the new statute. On February 8, 1974,
the district court dismissed the complaint without prejudice,
on non-jurisdictional grounds.

On February 6, 1974, the House of Representatives adopted House Resolution 803 which authorizes the Committee on the Judiciary to investigate the existence of grounds for the impeachment of President Nixon. The resolution also contains an express grant of subpoena power, but, of course, it does not have the status of a statute. 120 Cong. Rec. H 526 (daily ed., Feb. 6, 1974).

F. Applicability of Due Process

The Fifth Amendment provides in part: "No person shall be . . . deprived of life, liberty or property, without due process of law . . . ." Court decisions have interpreted due process as embodying standards of fairness, but the cases indicate that due process has many facets, depending upon the nature of the proceedings, i.e., criminal, civil, administrative. Standards applicable in one context may not be applicable in another. But whether or not capable of judicial enforcement, due process standards would seem to be relevant to the manner of conducting an impeachment proceeding.

The rules of the Congress cover some issues. One type of issue relates to the ability of the President to be represented at the inquiry of the House Committee, to cross-examine witnesses, and to offer witnesses and evidence. There do not appear to be House rules dealing with such matters, but an annotation in Jefferson's Manual (§ 606) states that in the more recent impeachment inquiries by House committees, the accused has been permitted to be present, to be represented by counsel, to present witnesses and to cross-examine. Similar procedures are expressly set forth in the Senate rules regarding impeachment.

An unresolved issue concerns the conduct of members of the House and of the Senate in commenting publicly upon impeachment. Pertinent in this regard are the fundamental differences between judicial proceedings and impeachment.

The rules governing criminal cases are such that a conviction by a judge who, before the trial, had expressed his belief that the defendant was guilty would be invalid. Similarly, the members of a petit jury must be impartial, and an indictment may be challenged on the ground of improper grand jury selection.

The function of the House in regard to impeachment is similar to that of a grand jury; and the functions of the Senate resemble those of a judge (determining legal issues) and a jury (determining factual issues) in a criminal trial. However, there are limits to these analogies, for by its nature impeachment differs from judicial proceedings.

The decision of the Framers to place the trial of impeachments in the Senate (rather than in a court) necessarily has meant that impeachments have an extra - judicial political aspect, whether consciously intended or not. The Framers perhaps had in mind an analogy to the judicial role of the House of Lords, but our developed governmental system is quite different.

G. Judicial Review of Impeachments

The issue discussed in this part is whether a person convicted by the Senate may obtain court review of the conviction.

Apparently, none of the four judges who was convicted in impeachment proceedings sought direct review of his conviction and removal. However, Judge Halsted L. Ritter brought an action in the Court of Claims for back salary.[23/] Ritter claimed that the Senate had exceeded its jurisdiction in that it had tried him on charges which did not constitute impeachable offenses under the Constitution. The Court of Claims disclaimed jurisdiction on the ground that the Senate's power and jurisdiction were exclusive with reference to impeachment. Citing Mississippi v. Johnson, 71 U.S. 475 (1866), the Court of Claims stated that the impeachment power, being vested in the Senate and the House, was essentially "political" and not subject to judicial review.[24/]

23/ Ritter v. United States, 84 Ct. Cl. 293 (1936), cert. denied, 300 U.S. 668 (1937).

24/ In the Brief for the United States in Opposition to Certiorari, Solicitor General Reed stated that the decision of the Court of Claims that it had no jurisdiction to look behind the impeachment judgment was "clearly correct." Relying on the terms and history of the Constitution, the Solicitor General maintained that "impeachment proceedings are committed exclusively to Congress."

Until recently, the view that impeachment convictions were not subject to judicial review was generally accepted. However, Berger and two other recent writers[25] take the opposite position. Berger's views may be summarized as follows: The Framers did not intend to deliver the President (or judges) to the "unbounded discretion of Congress." The Constitution limits the grounds for impeachment, and a conviction whose basis exceeds those bounds might constitute a denial of Due Process. Such issues as the meaning of "high crimes and misdemeanors" are properly resolved by the courts. Powell v. McCormack, 395 U.S. 486 (1969), is a close analogy and indicates that the "political question" doctrine is not an obstacle to judicial review of an impeachment conviction.

Berger's conclusion and his treatment of the history of the Constitution may be questioned. The Framers rejected plans to place the trial of impeachments in the Supreme Court or another court. Notwithstanding the contrary view of Berger, the apparent reasons for rejecting a judicial role in the trial of impeachments (e.g., the political nature

---

25/ See Brant, Impeachment, Trials and Errors (1972); Feerick, Impeaching Federal Judges, 39 Fordham L. Rev. 1 (1970); Berger, Impeachment (1973).

of the impeachment process) may also apply to review of impeachment convictions. Cf. _Ritter_ v. _United States_, _supra_. During state ratification debates, various checks on the impeachment power were mentioned (e.g., the two-stage process, the role of the Chief Justice as presiding officer when a President is being tried, the fact that members of Congress are accountable to the electorate). There appears to be no record, however, of any statement (at the Constitutional Convention or the ratification conventions) to the effect that judicial review of impeachment convictions would be available. It is true, of course, that the institution of judicial review in its present vigor was not clearly perceived and discussed at the time of the Constitutional Convention.

The issue of the meaning of impeachable offenses would seem to be more "political" or subjective in nature than was the question presented in _Powell_ v. _McCormack_ (i.e., the power of the House to exclude an elected representative for reasons unrelated to the qualifications set forth in Article I).

In short, given the history of the Constitution, the nature of impeachment, the decision in the _Ritter_ case, and the traditional view held by many scholars, Berger's view that generally speaking the merits of an impeachment conviction are subject to judicial review is distinctly a minority position. An argument can be made that the Constitution commits to Congress the meaning of "high crimes and misdemeanors," and that as a general matter no judicial review is available, though the Powell case raises a question mark. There may be a role for the courts at least in certain limited circumstances -- e.g., an impeachment and conviction by House and Senate votes alone, without any factual inquiry into an impeachable offense, thus raising both jurisdictional and Due Process questions; or a Senate judgment exceeding the sanctions of removal and disqualification, again raising a question of constitutional jurisdiction.

There are also practical difficulties with judicial review. One question is whether a statutory basis for direct judicial review (as opposed to a back-pay suit such as Ritter v. United States, supra) exists. Also it would be perilous to have the President's title to office in suspension, and the Vice President's status in doubt, in the period after an impeachment conviction and prior to completion of judicial review. Further, if the Chief Justice, having presided

at the Senate trial, felt he had to recuse himself from

Supreme Court review, a tie vote in the Court could result.

H. Effect of Resignation Upon Impeachment Proceedings

As a practical matter, if the President should resign, this would probably result in termination of impeachment proceedings.

The legal issue is not clear. Some scholars, e.g., Story, have maintained that a person holding no "office" or no longer holding office is beyond the scope of the impeachment power. This view asserts that the primary thrust of impeachment is to remove an offending official from his office. The opposing view rests on the fact that removal is not the sole sanction, that a person convicted in impeachment proceedings may also be disqualified from holding "any office of honor, trust or profit under the United States."

The impeachment of William W. Belknap in 1876 continued despite the fact that, just before the House adopted a resolution impeaching him, he had resigned from his office of Secretary of War. Still, a major reason for his acquittal was doubt as to the jurisdiction of the Senate. Also, Senator Blount, whose case was dismissed in 1798 by the Senate on other grounds, had been expelled by the Senate prior to his impeachment. In other cases (e.g., Judge English), resignation was followed by the cessation of impeachment proceedings.

Department of Justice

FOR RELEASE AT 6:00 P.M., EDT
FRIDAY, FEBRUARY 22, 1974

THE LAW OF IMPEACHMENT

Appendix I: The Concept of Impeachable Offense

Department of Justice
Washington, D.C. 20530

February 21, 1974

The attached Appendices I and II, discussing the historical background of the impeachable offense concept are part of research on the legal aspects of impeachment undertaken by the Office of Legal Counsel. These are working papers.

This material is a general academic discussion, without reference to any particular factual allegations. It does not reach conclusions or propose solutions. It is resource material.

Robert G. Dixon, Jr.
Assistant Attorney General
Office of Legal Counsel

This appendix is an interim working paper prepared by the staff of the Office of Legal Counsel. The views expressed should not be regarded as an official position of the Department of Justice.

Some of the views set forth here may, as the result of further research, be subject to modification.

Robert G. Dixon, Jr.
Assistant Attorney General
Office of Legal Counsel

Appendix I

THE CONCEPT OF IMPEACHABLE OFFENSE
HISTORICAL DERIVATION AND AMERICAN PRECEDENTS

A. Introduction:

The primary guides to the concept of impeachable offense are the historical derivation of the Constitutional provision and the impeachment and attempted impeachment proceedings which have occurred. We do not purport to analyze or evaluate the various allegations concerning the President and his Administration which, as reported in the press, enter into the public discussion concerning the definition of an impeachable offense.

Article II, section 4 of the Constitution provides that "[t]he President, Vice President and all civil officers of the United States, shall be removed from Office on Impeachment for, and conviction of, Treason, Bribery, or other high Crimes and Misdeameanors." The terms treason and bribery describe specific offenses defined in the criminal and common law (cf. 18 U.S.C. 201, 2381). Treason is also defined in Article III, section 3, clause 1 of the Constitution.

Debate has centered over the content to be given to the phrase "other high Crimes and Misdemeanors." This discussion focuses on those words. "Crimes" and "misdemeanors" are, of course, familiar terms in the criminal law today. Since they are placed in the same clause as treason and bribery, and since "conviction" is required for removal, one can make a strong argument, based on the text of the Constitution alone, that impeachment can only be predicated on a "high" criminal offense that deserves placement next to treason and bribery. [1] Also the word "other," linking back to treason and bribery, implies that the phrase "high Crimes and Misdemeanors" identifies further criminal offenses. Perhaps the best argument that can be made in favor of the narrow or criminal offense interpretation is that a "strict construction" of the language of the Constitution itself seems so clear that recourse to precedent and history is not necessary.

Related constitutional provisions seem to reinforce this conclusion. Article I, section 3 speaks of persons

---

[1] Of course, a textual problem is presented by the fact that "other high crimes" would suffice if this were intended, making the word "misdemeanors" surplusage, assuming "high" modifies both terms. Had the clause said "high felonies and misdemeanors" it would have been more consistent with this argument. See A. Simpson, Federal Impeachments, 64 U. Pa. L. Rev. 651, 679 (1916).

- 4 -

"convicted" by the Senate on trial of impeachment. The same section provides that the party "convicted" shall be subject to indictment and punishment, a possibility that would not exist, of course, unless the charges were criminal to begin with. Similarly, the President has power to pardon for "Offences against the United States, except in Cases of Impeachment" (Art. II, §2). Moreover, "The Trial of all Crimes, except in Cases of Impeachment, shall be by Jury" (Art. III, §2). Thus all relevant clauses suggest the need for a criminal offense, [2] although, of course, they do not expressly forbid an additional non-criminal penumbra. As shown below in the discussion of American precedents, the view that the constitutional text suggests the need for a criminal offense has been argued in the past with some success. For example, one of Andrew Johnson's counsel stated at his trial:

2/ This theory is, with some qualification, accepted by one of the most recent books on the subject -- Impeachment: Trials and Errors by Irving Brant (Knopf 1972), p. 23 ("Brant"). There is an alternative argument for the narrow view based on the idea that English practice was incorporated into the Constitution and that "it is settled in England that an impeachment is only * * * for an indictable offence." Pomeroy, Constitutional Law 601 (10th ed., 1898). As is shown in some detail below, any assumptions regarding English law are subject to great debate.

In my apprehension, the teachings, the
requirements, the prohibitions of the Constitution of the United States prove all that is
necessary to be attended to for the purposes
of this trial. I propose, therefore, instead
of a search through the precedents which were
made in the times of the Plantagenets, the
Tudors, and the Stuarts, and which have been
repeated since, to come nearer home and see
what provisions of the Constitution of the
United States bear on this question, and
whether they are not sufficient to settle it.
If they are, it is quite immaterial what exists
elsewhere.

Proceedings in the Trial of Andrew Johnson before the

United States Senate on Articles of Impeachment (F.J. Rives

& Geo. A. Bailey, Washington, 1868), pp. 273-74 (hereinafter

"Trial of Andrew Johnson").

However, as soon as one turns to the background

of the Impeachment Clause, and the precedents set under

it, the matter becomes far more complicated. There are

historical precedents and writings showing a broad

definition. $\underline{3}/$ And yet when this material is subjected

to analysis the conclusions to be derived become qualified

or uncertain.

$\underline{3}/$ See, e.g., Committee on Federal Legislation, Association
of the Bar of the City of New York, The Law of Presidential
Impeachment (N.Y., 1974).

Statements abound that impeachment is a prophylactic remedy to protect the public interest and not to punish. For example, in the opening remarks of the very first such proceeding, involving Senator Blount, it was said:

> * * * impeachment is a proceeding purely of a political nature. It is not so much designed to punish an offender as to secure the State. It touches neither his person nor his property, but simply divests him of his political capacity. 8 Annals of Congress 2251 (1798).

Bearing in mind that this may be the agreed purpose of impeachment, it would follow that the "criminality" requirement would neither be necessary not desirable as a way of protecting the public. Under this hypothesis, one can conceive of serious abuses of power which have not been made crimes. Story has said, "The silence of the statute-book" should not be permitted to make the impeachment power "a complete nullity." Joseph Story, Commentaries on the Constitution of the United States, §796, vol. 1 (Little, Brown & Co., 4th ed., 1873). The answer, in part, is that it is 140 years since Story originally wrote these words in 1833, and he was not summarizing a universal understanding at that time. Criminal jurisdiction has grown enormously so that the idea of restricting impeachments to criminal offenses would not be as limiting as before.

Despite the purpose of only "securing the State" rather than punishing the offender, the feeling of many citizens and many members of Congress is that impeachment of a President is, if anything, more serious than an ordinary criminal trial, "an almost parricidal act", [4] and that strict standards should be applied. Moreover as argued in a case early in this century:

> * * * notwithstanding what some text writers have said, I venture the assertion that if you go out into the cars or on the streets or in your homes and ask the people you meet what is meant by the words "treason, bribery, or other high crimes and misdemeanors," you will not find one in a thousand but will say that every one of those words imports a crime. [5]

---

[4] Raoul Berger, Impeachment: An Instrument of Regeneration, Harper's, January 1974, p. 14.

[5] Statement of Alexander Simpson on behalf of Judge Archbald, 6 Cannon's Precedents of the House of Representatives, 646 (hereinafter "Cannon").

A review of historical material follows. Parts B, C and D deal with the historical derivation of the Constitutional provision. Part E considers the impeachment proceedings which have taken place in this country.

If there is one lesson to be learned from this material it is that nothing can be considered resolved concerning the concept of impeachable offenses. The same basic arguments are repeated in each succeeding proceeding.

B. The Constitutional Convention of 1787:

The available records of the Convention indicate that
the term "high Crimes and Misdemeanors" was not intended
to be completely open-ended but do not teach us a great
deal more. The reader should understand that our
perception of what debate occurred at the Convention is
based largely on notes of participants, principally Madison,
which do not approximate the completeness or accuracy of
present day records. 6/

A number of different plans for impeachment provisions
were put forth by various delegations at the end of May
1787. A first decision, though not a final one, was made
early in the Convention. A motion was adopted to add to
the article on executive power, a provision for the executive
"to be removable on impeachment & conviction of mal-practice
or neglect of duty." 1 Farrand, The Records of the Federal
Convention of 1787 88 (1937 revised ed.) (hereinafter
"Farrand"). Subsequently there was discussion as to whether

6/ A more comprehensive description of the Convention as
it relates to all clauses relating to impeachment will be
found elsewhere in Appendix II. See also J.E. Kallenbach,
The American Chief Executive 51-56 (1966); J.D. Feerick,
Impeaching Federal Judges: A Study of the Constitutional
Provisions, 39 Fordham L. Rev. 1, 15-23 (1970) ("Feerick").

the President should be subject to impeachment at all. An unsuccessful effort was made to delete the clause providing for the removal of the President. On July 20, a debate took place concerning impeachment of the President. Varying reasons were given for having such a provision as well as for omitting it. The discussion suggested that matters not criminal or necessarily criminal in nature could be impeachable. Thus such grounds as "negligence," "incapacity," and "oppression" were mentioned. In addition some bases for impeachment, more likely to be criminal, such as "corruption" and "peculation" were brought up. 2 Farrand at 64-69. The Convention then agreed again to the clause (previously adopted while sitting as the Committee of the Whole) with impeachment grounds given as "malpractice or neglect of duty." 2 Farrand at 61 and 69. On July 26, the Convention reaffirmed this definition. 2 Farrand 116.

The decisions made up to that point were referred to a Committee of Detail which drafted and presented its report. The committee's report provided that the President could be impeached for "treason, bribery, or corruption." 2 Farrand 185-86. A subsequent report of a different committee limited the grounds further to either "Treason, or bribery." 2 Farrand 499.

The impeachment provisions were taken up again by the Convention on September 8. The limitation of impeachment to "Treason & bribery" was questioned. 2 Farrand 550. It was noted that treason, as defined in the Constitution, would not reach many great and dangerous offenses, nor would attempts to subvert the Constitution be covered. Col. Mason proposed therefore to add "maladministration" as a ground for impeachment. However, Madison said that so vague a term as "maladministration" would be equivalent to placing the tenure of the President "during pleasure of the Senate." Gouverneur Morris said that an election every four years would suffice to prevent maladministration. In light of this criticism, Madison's notes show that the term "maladministration" was withdrawn and the words "other high crimes & misdemeanors" were substituted and adopted. 2 Farrand 550.

From the Convention notes some conclusions can be argued:

(1) The term "high crimes and misdemeanors" meant something narrower than "maladministration." The notion that a President could be removed at the pleasure of the Senate simply if there were enough votes was rejected. 7/

_____

7/ However, our only Presidential impeachment (continued)

However, there is no specific record of any discussion of what it did, in fact, mean. As far as we can tell, it was not used in the Convention in connection with impeachment until the end of the debate on the impeachment clause. However, the use of the words high misdemeanors was proposed by the Committee of Detail and then rejected in connection with the Extradition Clause (Art. IV) where it was recognized as having a limited, technical meaning. 2 Farrand 174, 443; Berger 74. What was meant by limited and technical is not shown in the records available. However, the fact that the Committee recommended the words in connection with extradition in the first instance shows a criminal law connotation.

(2) Although there was a passing reference at the Convention to the impeachment of Warren Hastings of the British East India Company, which was then pending in England (2 Farrand 550), there is no documentable intent to adopt

---

7/ (cont'd) to date, that of President Andrew Johnson, has been viewed as an example of this very thing. If there is no judicial review--a matter never definitively resolved--congressional votes could end the matter. An example of this perspective is the statement of Attorney General Kleindienst that a President can be removed without evidence merely by obtaining enough votes. See Executive Privilege, Hearings Before the Subcommittee on Intergovernmental Relations of the Senate Government Operations Committee et al., 93d Cong., 1st Sess., vol. 1, p. 52 (1973).

English practice and precedent on impeachment.

(3) Most of the recorded discussion at the Convention, on which suggested that impeachment would be available for non-criminal offenses, took place some six weeks before the adoption of the term "high crimes and misdemeanors." The Framers seem to have been offering reasons for impeachment rather than definitions of impeachable offenses. At that time the phrase before the Convention was "malpractice or neglect of duty," clearly a much broader definition than the final text. In the absence of any direct discussion of the final wording, one could argue that the text itself should be relied on as the main source of interpretation.

It might be said, of course, that those who six weeks before had advocated a broader clause would have objected if they thought that the language finally adopted did not meet their intentions. However, it is just as logical to assume that they were, as the end of the summer in Philadelphia neared, more ready to compromise. There were, as noted, those who supported even narrower grounds, such as "treason and bribery" and those who thought that an impeachment provision was not necessary at all.

One therefore must read with care writers who make

rather free use of quotations from early in the Convention,
such as "negligence" and "perfidy," to show what the final
definition means. See, e.g., Anthony Lewis, "Negligence
or Perfidy", _N.Y. Times_, December 10, 1973, p. 37; and
Berger, p. 89.

C. Post-Convention Statements:

In the period following the Convention statements were made which are often cited as casting light on the meaning of the impeachment clause.

1. Ratifying conventions.

The state ratifying conventions might be given weight. Indeed, it could be argued that the views of the ratifiers are more relevant than what was said at the Convention. The records of the Convention were secret at the time of ratification by the states. It can be said that it was the Constitution as understood by the Ratifiers that was adopted.

It should be recognized, however, that there is no sustained analysis of impeachment in the ratification debates. Fairly complete records exist for only a few state conventions. One cannot assume therefore that what is available represents a universal understanding. This furnishes an additional reason for reliance on the constitutional text itself. (A more comprehensive discussion of the state ratifying conventions can be found in Appendix II).

Some clues do emerge however. One idea put forward was the concept that impeachable offenses must be "great" ones. James Iredell, later a Supreme Court Justice, said of impeachment in the North Carolina Convention that "the occasion for its exercise will arise from acts of great injury to the community." 4 Elliot, <u>The Debates in the Several State Conventions on the Adoption of the Federal Constitution</u> 113 (1836) (hereinafter "Elliot"). Another North Carolina delegate said that impeachment "is a mode of trial pointed out for great misdemeanors against the public." 4 Elliot 48. <u>8</u>/

However, there were other statements, showing a variety of ideas as to what impeachable offenses were. For example, Madison said in the Virginia Convention that "if the President be connected, in any suspicious manner, with any person, and there be grounds to believe he will shelter him," he may be impeached. He also said that were the President to commit anything so atrocious as to summon only a few states to consider a treaty he would be impeached for a misdemeanor. 3 Elliot 498, 500. In North Carolina, Iredell said, "I suppose the only instances, in

---

<u>8</u>/ Based on this Berger repeatedly makes the point that impeachment of a President can only be for a "great offense." See pp. 88, 124, 146, 162, 163.

which the President would be liable to impeachment, would be where he had received a bribe, or had acted from some corrupt motive or other." 4 Elliot 126. Delegates in South Carolina said that those are impeachable who behave amiss or betray or abuse public trust. 4 Elliot 276, 281.

Many of those remarks describe the impeachment power in terms which were broad enough to include criminal conduct, but which did not necessarily require it. This would be true of such words as "abuse of trust." And certainly, there was a recognition given that impeachment could be brought for disregard of the accepted processes of government even though no crime be committed. A good example is Madison's hypothetical concerning summoning only a few states in order to secure approval for a treaty.

2. The Federalist

A leading source of constitutional interpretation is The Federalist, a collection of essays, primarily by Madison and Hamilton, whose purpose was to explain and support the newly drafted Constitution at the time that it was being considered by the states. It was carried in the newspapers of the day and thus, in theory, available to the ratifiers. We do not, however, find it being cited in the state conventions.

In _Federalist No. 65_, Hamilton discussed impeachment and gave the reasons for the Senate being chosen as the forum for trying impeachments. Indirectly he cast light on the nature of what was considered impeachable:

> The subjects of its jurisdiction are those offenses which proceed from the misconduct of public men, or, in other words, from the abuse or violation of some public trust. They are of a nature which may with peculiar propriety be denominated POLITICAL, as they relate chiefly to injuries done immediately to the society itself. (_The Federalist_, The Central Law Journal Co., St. Louis, 1914, vol. 2, p. 17.)

Hamilton also noted that an impeachment case "can never be tied down by such strict rules * * * in the delineation of the offense by the prosecutors, or in the construction of it by the judges, as in common cases serve to limit the discretion of courts in favor of personal security." _Id._ at 19. He speaks also of "The awful discretion which a court of impeachments must necessarily have" as a reason for not giving the power to try impeachments to the Supreme Court. _Ibid._ Hamilton's analysis is the most systematic exegesis of the impeachment provisions that we have from the ratification period. It makes clear that an impeachment proceeding would be likely to have factional animosities (Id. at 17) and because of the great discretion involved was quite different in its jurisdictional aspects and tenor from the cases brought in the ordinary courts. Instead, impeachments are broadly aimed at abuses of the public trust. This, of course, cuts against any argument for a narrow definition of high crimes and misdemeanors limited to criminal offenses.

3. The First Congress.

Statements made at the First Congress are often cited as being authoritative on the meaning of the Constitution. Under conventional notions of construction statements made subsequent to an enactment by individuals in Congress ordinarily are to be discounted. Nevertheless, both writers and the courts have recognized that the construction given to the Constitution in the First Congress is entitled to particular weight because it included persons both from the Convention which framed the Constitution and from the state conventions which had adopted it. E.g., Berger 283-284, and cases cited. At the same time, the decisions and views of the First Congress are not always

conclusive on constitutional points. <u>Fairbank</u> v. <u>United</u>
<u>States</u>, 181 U.S. 283, 306-312 (1901).

Some of the statements often cited as defining what
is impeachable were made in the First Congress. They were
made in a debate on the question whether the President had
the right to remove executive officers. Incident to this,
references were made to impeachment proceedings. Arguing
for the President's right to remove officers by himself,
Madison said:

> I think it absolutely necessary that the
> President should have the power of removing
> from office; it will make him, in a peculiar
> manner, responsible for their conduct, and
> subject him to impeachment himself, if he
> suffers them to perpetrate with impunity
> high crimes or misdemeanors against the United
> States, or neglects to superintend their conduct,
> so as to check their excesses. 1 Annals of
> Congress 372-373; see also <u>id</u>. at 380.

Madison also said, concerning the advisability of empowering

the President to remove executive officers:

> The danger, then, consists merely in this: the
> President can displace from office a man whose
> merits require that he should be continued in
> it. What will be the motives which the
> President can feel for such abuse of his power
> and the restraints that operate to prevent it?
> In the first place, he will be impeachable by
> this House before the Senate for such an act
> of maladministration; for I contend that the
> wanton removal of meritorious officers would
> subject him to impeachment and removal from his
> own high trust. <u>Id</u>. at 498.

One might point out that this latter statement does not
appear to be consistent with what Madison's own notes
show that he himself said at the Convention. As
indicated, _supra_, he objected at the Convention to impeachment for "maladministration" since this would amount to
the President serving at the pleasure of the Senate.
Since many people are asked to resign posts who can be
said by someone to have merit, the example could be advanced
to prove the validity of Madison's objection to impeachment for "maladministration." Such "wanton removal" could be
accomplished in a criminal context, of course, such as a
conspiracy to obstruct justice. Nevertheless, this post-
convention remark by Madison can be cited in support of
the contention that conduct that is neither criminal nor
a violation of law might be considered impeachable. 9 /

---

9 / Compare, however, the analysis of Brant, p. 22, who
argues that the context of Madison's remark shows that
"criminality" would be required.

D. The Relevance of British Precedent:

As indicated, examination of the records of the Federal
Convention of 1787, supra, reveals no attempt to explain
the derivation of the words "high Crimes and Misdemeanors."
In the state ratifying conventions there were several
references to the English practice. However, they fall
considerably short of indicating an intention to incor-
porate British practice regarding the definition of an
impeachable offense. In The Federalist, Hamilton
referred to the British "model" of having one House prosecute and the other sit as jury, and described the use of
impeachment in England as a "bridle" (Federalist No. 65,
vol. 2, p. 18). However, one does not have to assume that
he was doing more than drawing analogies and justifying
the exceptions to the separation of powers found in the
American constitutional provisions relating to impeachment.

One might certainly conclude that in adopting a
Constitution of limited powers the Framers reacted to and
rejected some precedents in British law generally and the
impeachment area specifically.[10/] Brant, p. 13, 41-42. For
example, Kallenbach writes:

_____

10/ British practice itself, however, varied over the
centuries, as discussed in Appendix II.

> By limiting its use to public officers, by
> defining with some particularity the grounds
> upon which impeachment charges might be based,
> and by limiting the punishment that might be
> imposed to separation from office and possible
> disqualification from officeholding in the
> future, the Framers converted this ancient de-
> vice for special trial into an instrument for
> disciplining public officers by removal from
> office for misconduct. J. Kallenbach, The
> American Chief Executive 51 (1966).

A nineteenth centry text goes further:

> we must reject the interpretation which makes
> impeachment under the Constitution co-extensive
> only with impeachment as it practically exists
> in England. The word is borrowed, the procedure
> is imitated, and no more; the object and end of
> the process are far different. Pomeroy,
> Constitutional Law 608 (10th Ed. 1888).

In related areas, in deviation from British practice, the

Framers had prohibited bills of attainder (which involved

legislative punishment with no trial at all), prohibited

ex post facto laws and limited the definition of treason

which had been subject to abuse (Berger 54-55). Subse-

quently, for similar reasons, both the Due Process Clause

and Free Speech Clauses were adopted.

In the first impeachment trial, that of William

Blount in 1798, the issue was raised as to the relevance

of following English precedent. The House Manager had

claimed that the English practice of impeaching private

citizens could be followed by the American Congress. 8 Annals of Cong. 2254, 2291 ff. In reply, defense counsel pointed out that the Constitution did not expressly adopt the common law and that it was questionable whether precedent should be taken "from the dark and barbarous pages of the common law, with all the feudal rigor and appendages." Id. at 2264. In fact counsel cited a variety of cases to show the "extravagant length to which the ancient common law doctrine of impeachments had been extended." Id. at 2265. He argued that "the Constitution presents a complete and consistent system:--it declares who shall impeach, who shall try, who may be impeached, for what offences, and how the delinquents shall be punished." Id. at 2268. The English precedent was implicitly rejected since the charge was dismissed. 3 Hind's Precedents of the House of Representatives 679 (1907) (hereinafter "Hind") (references are to pages except where sections are designated).

Counsel for Andrew Johnson noted the contrast in the two forms of Government--English and American. He referred to the fact that some of the articles voted by

the House based on Johnson's speeches violated the First
Amendment:

> That is the same freedom of speech, Senators,
> in consequence of which thousands of men went
> to the scaffold under the Tudors and the
> Stuarts. Trial of Andrew Johnson, p. 277.

Despite this American background, it has been assumed or
argued by writers that the words of the impeachment
clause are derived from British law and that one should
thus rely on British practice. This is a major thesis of
Berger's recent book.

Berger traces the phrase "high Crimes and Misdemeanors"
to an impeachment proceeding in 1386 (pp. 59, 61). He
shows that the term did not exist at that time in the
ordinary criminal law and concludes that high crimes and
misdemeanors appear to be words of art confined to
impeachments. Berger 61-62.

How much detailed knowledge of English history one
can impute to the Framers is uncertain even if the
assumption that they consciously referred to English
practice is valid. Berger lists a number of impeachments
(pp. 67-69) whose source is given as Howell's State Trials,

published in London 1809-1826, after the Convention.
Berger 316. At the same time he provides evidence
regarding the general availability of English materials
to the Framers and the fact that some had studied in
England. Berger 87.

The British precedents compiled by Berger show that
impeachments were brought for matters that were not
crimes and perhaps did not even violate any clear legal
standard. Nonetheless, the charges often recited that
such matters constituted high crimes and misdemeanors.
In 1626 the Duke of Buckingham was charged, among other
things, with the fact that though young and inexperienced,
he procured offices for himself, thereby blocking the
deserving. Berger 68.

A number of precedents do charge violation of some
official duty or norm. For example, a Lord Treasurer
allowed the office of ordnance to go unrepaired though
money was appropriated for that purpose and he allowed
contracts for greatly needed powder to lapse for want of
payment. A Commissioner of the Navy was charged in 1668
with negligent preparation for the Dutch invasion and
with loss of a ship through neglect to bring it to mooring.

A Chief Justice discharged a grand jury before it made its presentments thereby obstructing the presentments. A mayor of London was charged with thwarting Parliament's order to store arms and ammunition in storehouses. Ibid.

Berger notes that the charges are reducible to intelligible categories including misapplication of funds, abuse of official power, neglect of duty, encroachment on or contempt of the prerogatives of Parliament, corruption, betrayal of trust and giving pernicious advice to the Crown. These precedents establish that it was unnecessary under English law for an act to be a criminal or even a non-criminal violation of existing law to be a high crime or misdemeanor. He states that these categories may be taken to outline the boundaries of the phrase "high Crimes and Misdemeanors" at the time of the Convention. (pp. 70-71).

Although this may be true of British practice, the conclusion does not necessarily follow that the Framers meant to give the phrase the same content. Much of what the Framers did was a reaction against rather than a copy of the British model.

Further, Berger concedes that the phrase "high Crimes

and Misdemeanors" was to be given a "limited", "technical" meaning. Berger 71, 298.   As we have seen, _supra_, from the history of the clause at the Convention, "maladministration," a term which would have covered many of the British precedents, was rejected.

Moreover, even the English background, as it may have been perceived in Philadelphia in 1787 is not all that clear. We have not made an independent examination of the British precedents. However Simpson, an authority on impeachments, pointed out the difficulty of deciding which British precedents to select, if one decided that they were relevant at all, noting that the more recent impeachments required an indictable offense:

> the question arises which of the English
> precedents are you going to accept, in view
> of the fact that some hold that an impeach-
> able offense need not be an indictable one, and
> others hold a precisely antagonistic view.
> Are you going back to the days when a man
> was impeached simply because he happened to
> have been put in office by those who have
> themselves just been turned out? If that
> is the view you are going to accept then
> perhaps every four years in this country
> there will be a wholesale slaughter. But
> if you are going to accept the best

> precedents which appear upon the English reports,
> and especially those down near to the time when
> the Constitution of the United States was adopted,
> then those best precedents show that, except for
> an indictable offense, no impeachment would lie
> under the laws of England. 6 Cannon 646. 11/

Berger concedes that the view that impeachment must rest

upon a violation of existing criminal law "has the imprimatur

of Blackstone." Berger 55. Perhaps the best known and most

accessible source of English common law in the United States

was Blackstone's Commentaries on the Laws of England, pub-

lished some twenty years before the Federal Convention.

Other English pre-Convention sources agreed with the criminal-

violation concept. Berger 56. See also Pomeroy, Constitu-

tional Law 601 (10th ed. 1888). Thus, even if Berger is

technically correct in showing that Blackstone and others

had not stated British historical precedent correctly, the

fact that such well known contemporaneous commentators

embraced the restrictive interpretation may well have

influenced the Framers, assuming they considered the matter

at all. 12/

11/ Statement by Simpson while acting as counsel for Judge
Archbald in an impeachment trial in 1913. But see Simpson,
Federal Impeachments, 64 U.Pa.L.Rev. 651, 683-86 (1916).

12/ Cf. W. Bates, Vagueness in the Constitution: The Impeachment Power, 25 Stanford L. Rev. 908, 911 n. 22 (1973).

It may be inappropriate therefore to swallow "true"
English history whole as part of our Constitution, 13/
and ignore the Founding Father's understanding of it.

13/ Compare the minority views (5-4) of the Judiciary
Committee considering the impeachment of Andrew Johnson:

 The idea that the House of Representatives may
impeach a civil officer of the United States for any
and every act for which a parliamentary precedent
can be found is too preposterous to be seriously
considered. 3 Hind 840.

E. American Impeachment Precedents:

Perhaps the most important source of law concerning impeachment is the experience of Congress in conducting impeachment proceedings. 14/ The Houses of Congress look primarily to their own precedents--the practical construction of the Constitution. There have been twelve impeachments voted by the House. 15/ All have involved Federal judges with the exception of President Andrew Johnson (1868), Secretary of War William Belknap (1876),

---

14/ There are a number of stray judicial dicta which relate to the scope of impeachable offenses. However, they do not appear to be carefully considered nor have they arisen from impeachment proceedings. Compare Kilbourn v. Thompson, 103 U.S. 168, 193 (1880) (suggesting that in the absence of "criminality" impeachment could not be brought) with Ex parte Grossman, 267 U.S. 87, 121 (1925) (suggesting that excessive use of the pardon power might be impeachable). See also The Legal Tender Cases, 79 U.S. 457, 535 (1870) (noting that impeachment is part of the power of Congress "to punish crime"); Langford v. United States, 101 U.S. 341, 343 (1879) (President may be impeached for "wrong-doing"). A majority of the texts indicate that high crimes and misdemeanors are not specifically limited to criminal conduct. Most do not attempt the kinds of distinctions made in this Appendix, particularly regarding the differences between judges and executive officers. For summaries of what the texts indicate see Feerick at 55 and Berger at 58.

15/ The articles of impeachment in the twelve cases which reached the Senate are set forth in Impeachment,Selected Materials, House Judiciary Comm. Print, 93d Cong. 1st Sess. 125 ff. (Oct. 1973).

and Senator William Blount (1797). Only four convictions have been obtained; no executive officer has ever been convicted.

The large number of proceedings against judges complicates assessment of their precedent value in a proceeding involving the President. It has generally been the expressed opinion of the House that judges can be impeached for lack of good behavior or misbehavior. The Constitution provides that Federal judges "shall hold their Offices during good Behaviour." Art. III, Sec. 1. These words are not specified among the grounds for impeachment set out in Article II, section 4. The notion that judges can be impeached for misbehavior has been criticized. E.g., Berger 132, 164; Feerick at 51-52. However, it is clear that the proceedings against judges have been strongly influenced by this factor. 16/ Matters that might not be considered high crimes and misdemeanors

---

16/ See "Memorandum Concerning the Congressional Impeachment Power as it Relates to the Federal Judiciary" by Bethel B. Kelley and Daniel G. Wyllie, reprinted in Legal Materials on Impeachment, House Committee Print, 91st Cong., 2d Sess. (Aug. 11, 1970), p. 6. The memorandum argues that judges can be impeached for misbehavior and reviews the precedents as they relate to this issue.

with regard to non-judicial officers have been included in the charges against judges. Judges have been formally charged with misbehavior as well as high crimes and misdemeanors. E.g., 6 Cannon 686 (Archbald); 80 Cong. Rec. 3486-88 (Ritter). However, no judge has been removed for misbehavior alone.

Furthermore, there is difficulty in weighing impeachment proceedings. A vote of the House to bring charges can be taken as a judgment that certain acts constitute high crimes and misdemeanors, if proven. However, as Hamilton pointed out a court of impeachments has an "awful discretion." Federalist No. 65, supra. Even if the facts were proven, a Senator could vote against conviction because removal from office was warranted. Special verdicts are not taken on separate issues, such as whether certain acts constitute impeachable offenses. 3 Hind § 2339.

Thus, failure to convict does not necessarily amount to a holding that the charges were not high crimes and misdemeanors. Attempts to read historical or political "holdings" into some of the acquittals may be legitimate exercises in analysis. However, they tend to be particularly debatable. A review of the precedents follows.

1. William Blount.

Blount, a U.S. Senator from Tennessee, was impeached in 1798 for high crimes and misdemeanors. He was charged with violating America's neutrality and the laws of the United States by conspiring to transfer to England Spanish territory in Florida and Louisiana while Spain and England were at war; with conspiring in violation of law to undermine the confidence of Indian tribes in an agent of the United States appointed to reside among them; with attempting to seduce another official from his duty and with attempting to foment certain tribes to disaffection toward the United States. 3 Hind § 2302. Blount was ordered by the Senate to be taken into custody until he posted bond. 3 Hind 647. The Senate dismissed the charges on the ground that Senators are not impeachable. 17/ 3 Hind § 2318. In his answer to the charges Blount's counsel noted that he had not been charged with having committed any "crime or misdemeanor." The answer went on to say that

---

17/ The Senate had previously expelled Blount for "a high misdemeanor entirely inconsistent with his public trust and duty as a Senator," based on the charge of seducing an agent among the Indians. This was not a statutory offense. In re Chapman, 166 U.S. 661, 670 (1897).

the courts of the States as well as those of the United States are competent to punish "crimes and misdemeanors" if they have been perpetrated. 3 Hind § 2310. It does not appear that Blount argued that the charges did not amount to indictable offenses. Perhaps this was because it might have undermined his principal and successful argument--that the Senate had no jurisdiction and that the courts could thus handle the matter.

2. <u>John Pickering</u>.

In 1804 U.S. District Court Judge Pickering was impeached for high crimes and misdemeanors in four articles. 3 Hind 682. Three articles referred to conduct in violation of law during a suit to condemn a ship and its cargo. It was charged that he returned the ship to its owner without obtaining a bond for the value of the ship and a certificate from its owner showing all duties paid as required by law, that he wrongfully refused to hear government testimony, and that "wickedly" intending to violate the law, he refused the Government's claim for an appeal from his decision. The last article charged that he was intoxicated and used profanity on the bench. 3 Hind 690. Pickering did not answer but his son produced evidence of his insanity. He was convicted on all four articles.

Thus, in the first impeachment conviction Pickering was

found on the first three articles to have violated the

law although these did not charge criminal offenses. In

being drunk and committing blasphemy on the bench, he can be

said to have abused his office. 18/

Most accounts refer to Pickering as being insane at

the time. Some Senators opposed admission of evidence

on this point on the ground that it would preclude con-

viction for high crimes and misdemeanors. This can be

said to have reflected the view that the proceedings were

criminal in nature and if such evidence were introduced the

requisite intent could not be found. However, the evidence

was admitted and he was nonetheless convicted and removed.

Feerick 27. This is consistent with the idea that the

purpose of impeachment is prophylactic in nature, designed

to protect the public rather than punish.

18/ Intemperance has been described as a misdemeanor.
3 Hind 800.

3. Samuel Chase.

In 1804 eight articles of impeachment were voted against Associate Supreme Court Justice Samuel Chase. Six concerned his actions while presiding on circuit at treason and sedition trials and two concerned addresses delivered to grand juries. 3 Hind 722-24. He was charged, inter alia, with permitting a juror to serve knowing that he had made up his mind prior to the trial; with refusing to admit certain evidence offered by the defense, and for arresting the defendant when only a summons should have been issued. (See Berger 224 ff. for political and historical detail.) The trial gave rise to debate as to what constituted an impeachable offense. Chase was represented by Luther Martin who had been a delegate at the Constitutional Convention. He argued that under the Constitution only an indictable offense was impeachable:

> There can be no doubt but that treason and bribery are indictable offenses. We have only to inquire, then, what is meant by high crimes and misdemeanors? What is the true meaning of the word "crime?" It is the breach of some law which renders the person who violates it liable to punishment. There can be no crime committed when no such law is violated.

* * *

> Thus it appears crimes and misdemeanors
> are the violations of a law exposing the
> person to punishment, and are used in
> contradistinction to those breaches of
> law which are mere private injuries, and
> only entitle the injured to a civil remedy.
> 3 Hind 762.

Martin also pointed out that all the provisions of the

Constitution relating to impeachment use criminal law

terminology. 3 Hind 767-68. Another of Chase's counsel

argued that it was important "to repel the wild idea that

a judge may be impeached and removed from office although

he has violated no law of the country, but merely on the

vague and changing opinions of right and wrong." 3 Hind

760.

The House Managers argued before the Senate that

impeachable offenses need not be indictable. Since the

Constitution restricts punishment to removal and dis-

qualification from office, it can be said to distinguish

between indictable and impeachable offenses. 3 Hind 739.

The Managers also took the position that judges could be

impeached for misbehavior some aspects of which may be

indictable and some not. 3 Hind 740. Despite the

"misbehavior" argument, the vote was on whether a high crime

or misdemeanor had been committed. 3 Hind 771.

Chase was acquitted on all charges. Justice
Douglas has stated the lesson of this trial to be that
"our tradition even bars political impeachments." Chandler
v. Judicial Council, 398 U.S. 74, 136 (dissenting opinion).
Other sources state that the acquittal was influenced by
the arguments that offenses must be indictable to be
impeachable. Corwin says that Chase's acquittal "went
far to affix this reading" until after the Civil War. The
Constitution of the United States, Analysis and Interpretation, S. Doc. No. 39, 86th Cong., 1st Sess. p. 557.
To the same effect see the Minority Report of the House
Judiciary Committee concerning President Johnson's proposed
impeachment (3 Hind 839):

> If this case establishes anything it is that
> an impeachment can not be supported by any
> act which falls short of an indictable crime
> or misdemeanor. This point was urged by the
> able counsel for Chase with great ability and
> pertinacity; and the force with which it was
> presented drove the managers of the House of
> Representatives to seek shelter under that
> clause of the Constitution which says: "The
> judges * * * shall hold their offices during
> good behavior."

As noted, counsel for Chase was one of the Framers. In
the first impeachment contested on the merits he and
co-counsel were able to make the argument sufficiently

- 40 -

well to "obscure" the issues. Berger 228.

4. James H. Peck.

Peck, a Federal district judge, was impeached in 1830 for "high misdemeanors." It was charged that he wrongfully convicted an attorney of contempt. The basis for the contempt was publication by the attorney of a reply to an article by the judge. 3 Hind § 2370. In respect to the impeachment clause, per se, the Managers clearly indicated that its "technical meaning" required an indictable offense, but they also felt that at least regarding judges a broader approach was preferable:

> If * * * it shall be decided that no offense, no conduct of an officer, unless it be a high crime and misdemeanor, within the technical meaning of these terms, and punishable by some known and existing criminal law, is impeachable, what would be the condition of our Government, and especially the judicial department? (3 Hind §2380) (Emphasis added.)

> A judicial misdemeanor consists * * * in doing an illegal act, colore officii, with bad motives, or in doing an act within the competency of the court or judge in some cases, but unwarranted in a particular case from the facts existing in that case, with bad motives. 3 Hind §2379.

The solution was to invoke the good behavior provision in Article III, applicable only to judges, to justify an impeachment for non-criminal matters. 3 Hind §2381.

Counsel for Peck argued that "guilty intention is the gist of impeachment" and that the acts charged were a mere error in judgment for which the judge was "not answerable either civilly much less criminally." 3 Hind 802. Peck was found not guilty of the high misdemeanor charged. 3 Hind § 2383.

5. West H. Humphreys.

In 1861, Humphreys, a United States district judge in Tennessee ceased holding court and acted as a judge for the Confederacy. The following year he was impeached in seven articles alleging high crimes and misdemeanors. The first charged that in violation of his oath and duties he endeavored "to incite revolt and rebellion" by declaring publicly the right of the people to renounce allegiance to the United States. Other articles charged similar acts, which resemble treason including conspiring to oppose the Government by force. 3 Hind 810-11. Humphreys did not answer the charges and was convicted and removed from office. 3 Hind 820. The case shows an instance of conviction for a very great offense involving matters that presumably would have been considered criminal had the point been raised.

6. Andrew Johnson.

The Johnson trial is the only impeachment of a President and an important precedent for this reason. [19]

In 1868 President Johnson was impeached in eleven articles for high crimes and misdemeanors, based largely on alleged violations of the Tenure of Office Act (14 Stat. 430) ("the Act"), [20] 3 Hind § 2420. The act required the Senate's consent to removal by the President of officials appointed by him. Johnson believed the Act unconstitutional and dismissed Secretary of War Stanton without Senate approval. The first article thus charged

---

[19] The first proposed impeachment of a President appears to have been against Tyler in 1843; the charges included a wide variety of matters such as "arbitrary, despotic, and corrupt abuse of the veto power," which were not criminal in nature. A move to appoint a committee to investigate the charges was defeated in the House. 3 Hind § 2398.

[20] There was an earlier attempt to impeach Johnson which did not receive the approval of the House. 3 Hind § 2399-2407. An investigation was made by the Judiciary Committee. Its report, which is extensive, shows close division on the scope of impeachable offenses. The majority of five, recommending impeachment, argued for a broad construction (3 Hind § 2405), while the minority of four, citing, inter alia, the literal language of the Constitution and the Chase trial, supra, argued that impeachment was limited to indictable offenses (3 Hind § 2406).

that Stanton's removal was unlawful as an intentional violation of the Constitution and the Act. The next seven articles were variations on the first. Article IX alleged that Johnson as Commander in Chief gave direct orders to a major general in violation of a statute requiring all military orders to pass through the General of the Army, which Johnson said was also unconstitutional. Article X charged that Johnson ridiculed Congress by intemperate harangues against it. The last article charged that Johnson had declared that the Thirty-Ninth Congress only represented part of the states and its laws were therefore not binding on him, and that in pursuance of this declaration and in violation of his oath of office, Johnson had attempted to prevent execution of various laws.

The Act made it a high misdemeanor punishable by fines and imprisonment to accept any appointment to any office or to pay or receive payment for performing functions contrary to its provisions. Sections 5 and 9, 14 Stat. 431 (1867). Johnson was charged in Art. VIII "with intent to unlawfully control disbursements" contrary to the Act. Moreover, several articles charged him with conspiracy to violate it. A general conspiracy law had been passed

on the same day as the Act became law. Rev. Stat. 5440,
14 Stat. 484.

An answer was filed by Johnson's counsel denying,
inter alia, that his actions violated the Act or the
Constitution, that the acts charged were high crimes and
misdemeanors, and noting that Articles X and XI,
relating to speeches, were protected by the constitutional
guaranty of freedom of speech. 3 Hind §2428; Trial of Andrew
Johnson 22.

In the opening address, the Managers of the House
argued before the Senate for a broad definition of impeachable offense which did not require criminal conduct or even
a violation of positive law:

> We define, therefore, an impeachable high
> crime or misdemeanor to be one in its nature or
> consequences subversive of some fundamental or
> essential principle of government or highly
> prejudicial to the public interest, and this
> may consist of a violation of the Constitution,
> of law, of an official oath, or of duty, by an
> act committed or omitted, or, without violating
> a positive law, by the abuse of discretionary
> powers from improper motives, or for any
> improper purpose. (Trial of Andrew Johnson, p. 58,
> emphasis in original deleted.)

The Managers referred to Madison's statement in the
First Congress, supra, regarding "wanton removal of

meritorious officers" as being grounds for impeachment (Ibid.) and described the English practice (Id. at 59 ff).

In answer, counsel for the President, in opening the defense, argued that, based on the language of the Constitution, impeachable offenses were "only, high criminal offenses against the United States, made so by some law of the United States existing when the acts complained of were done." Id. at 274:

> Noscitur a sociis. High crimes and mis-
> demeanors; so high that they belong in
> this company with treason and bribery.

It was argued that if every Senator was a law unto himself, able to declare an act criminal after its commission, then the ex post facto prohibition of the Constitution would be violated. Id. at 274-75. As to the Senate's duty, the defense said (Id. at 275):

> You must find that the law existed; you must
> construe it and apply it to the case; you
> must find his criminal intent willfully to
> break the law * * *.

The Senate voted first on Article XI, relating to Johnson's speech that the Congress did not represent all the States. Conviction failed by one vote short of the required two-thirds majority, 35-19. 3 Hind § 2440. Votes were later taken on two of the articles relating to the Tenure of Office Act and the same result was reached. No vote was taken on the remaining articles. 3 Hind §2443.

The trial has been described as "submerged in a quagmire of legal technicalities, focused upon the sole question of whether the President had committed a crime." T. Walthall, Executive Impeachment: Stealing Fire From the Gods, 9 N.E.L. Rev. 257, 291 (1974). Opinions were filed after the vote by individual Senators, some of which said that a crime was necessary for impeachment. Trial of Andrew Johnson 863-1090. See, e.g., opinion of Sen. Reverdy Johnson, id. at 887, 888 ("an officer can only be impeached for acts for which he is liable to a criminal prosecution."); Sen. James W. Grimes, id. at 870,875 ("I ask whether * * * the President's guilty intent to do an unlawful act 'shines with such a clear and certain light' as to justify * * * us to pronounce him guilty of a high constitutional crime or misdemeanor?") (emphasis in original).

It is difficult to say what the Johnson precedent stands for considering the difficulties of interpretation discussed, supra. However, Corwin, a noted writer on the

Presidency, says that with Johnson's acquittal, the narrow view of "high crimes and misdemeanors" appeared to win out. The Constitution of the United States of America, Analysis and Interpretation, S. Doc. No. 170, 82nd Cong., 2d Sess., p. 503. See also Corwin, The President: Office and Powers, 1787-1957, p. 353 (1957). Berger, who in general argues for a broad definition of impeachable offense, nevertheless describes the trial as "a gross abuse of the impeachment process, an attempt to punish the President for differing with and obstructing the policy of Congress." p. 295.

7. William W. Belknap.

Belknap, Secretary of War under Grant, was impeached in 1876. 3 Hind §2449. This is the only other impeachment of an executive officer apart from Johnson. He was charged in five articles with taking money for appointing a post trader at a military base. Ibid. The allegation resembles bribery and presumably would have been indictable. One article charged Belknap with criminally disregarding his duty. Belknap was acquitted although a majority voted to convict him. 3 Hind § 2467.

8. Charles Swayne.

Swayne, a district court judge in Florida, was

charged in 1903 with a variety of matters including making false claims against the government and signing false certificates of his expenses as a judge, appropriating for personal use a railroad car in the possession of a receiver appointed by him, and living outside his judicial district in violation of a statute which made it a "high misdemeanor" to do so (Rev. Stat. 551). 3 Hind 960. It seems clear that Swayne was accused of criminal offenses. The defense was based on the argument that the conduct did not occur while holding court and accordingly was not impeachable. 3 Hind 326-28. The House Managers, in reply, pointed to the absurdity in permitting a judge who had been convicted and imprisoned for forgery or embezzlement to remain in office because his conduct did not occur while on the bench. 3 Hind 328. 21/ They concluded that (3 Hind 340):

> our fathers adopted a Constitution under which official malfeasance and nonfeasance, and, in some cases, misfeasance, may be the subject of impeachment, although not made criminal by act of Congress, or so recognized by the common law of England or any State of the Union. They adopted impeachment as a means of removing men from office whose misconduct imperils the public safety and

---

21/ This argument might be even stronger in the case of a President, who this Department has stated to be immune from criminal prosecution while in office. In such a case the only remedy would be impeachment. There is, however, a body of opinion to the effect that impeachment is limited to acts performed in an official capacity. See generally Berger 193 ff. Berger suggests, however, that private conduct (continued)

Swayne was acquitted on all counts.

9. Robert W. Archbald.

Archbald, a member of the Commerce Court, was impeached in 13 articles in July 1912. He was charged formally by the House with misbehavior as well as high crimes and misdemeanors, 6 Cannon 686, a standard concededly applicable only to judges and not to executive officers (6 Cannon 650). In previous impeachments it had been argued that "misbehavior" was impeachable. However, it was not charged in the articles of impeachment and was used as an argument for conviction of charges of high crimes and misdemeanors. The issue of whether impeachment may be brought for less than indictable offenses was raised, 6 Cannon § 462, complicated, of course, by the "misbehavior" issue (48 Cong. Rec. 8702-05). Archbald had been charged with a wide variety of matters (see 48 Cong. Rec. 8706), which did not appear to be criminal or even violate positive law as such, but were arguably improper. See Brown, The Impeachment of the Federal Judiciary, 26 Harv. L. Rev. 684, 704-05 (1913). The third article, for example,

---

21/ (contd) by the President would not be impeachable. Id. at 196-97. But see W. Bates, Vagueness in The Constitution: The Impeachment Power, 25 Stan. L. Rev. 908, 915 (1973) and C. Rossiter, The American Presidency 35 (Harcourt, Brace & Co., 1956). Cf. 6 Cannon § 458.

charged that Archbald used his position to influence a coal company, owned by a railroad, then a litigant in court, to lease certain properties to Archbald and his friends in return for which he agreed to use the railroad to transport the products of the properties. Impeachment was said not to punish the individual but to protect the public "from injury at the hands of their own servants and to purify the public service." 6 Cannon 643. The defense argued that a criminal offense must be shown, based on the language of the Constitution and on the English precedents closest in time to the Convention of 1787. 6 Cannon 635, 646.

Archbald was found guilty on five articles. Following the vote a number of Senators filed opinions explaining their votes. The Senators' opinions serve to emphasize the difficulty of ascertaining the "holding" of an impeachment. As summarized by Feerick:

> Some stated that they thought criminality was the standard for removal; some only voted guilty where they thought the offenses, as proven, constituted "high crimes and misdemeanors," and had voted not guilty where the charge involved only misconduct. Others said that they had voted not guilty on charges in which proof of evil intent was lacking, and yet a few others said they had voted guilty on any charge involving less than good behavior. 39 Ford. L. Rev. at 42-43.

outside of the language of the Constitution
* * * there is no law which binds the Senate
in this case to-day except that law which is
prescribed by their own conscience * * *.
Each Senator must fix his own standard; and
the result of this trial depends on whether
or not these offenses * * * come within the
law laid down by the conscience of each
Senator for himself.   6 Cannon 634.

Subsequently, one of the House Managers wrote that "the

judgment of the Senate in this case has forever removed

from the domain of controversy the proposition that the

judges are only impeachable for the commission of crimes

or misdemeanors against the laws of general application."

Brown, The Impeachment of the Federal Judiciary, 26 Harv.

L. Rev. 684, 705 (1913).   However, because of the mis-

behavior theory on which the case was presented and

decided it cannot be said that its logic extends to

executive officers.

    10. George W. English.

    English, a district court judge, was impeached in

1926 for misbehavior and misdemeanors including some

matters which bordered on criminal offenses such as

accepting a cash gift from a receiver appointed by him

as well as other acts which apparently were not

indictable such as disbarring attorneys without

notice or hearing. See Feerick at 43. A House
Judiciary subcommittee stated that impeachable conduct
included, among other things, gross betrayals of the
public interest, tyrannical abuse of power, and
inexcusable neglect of duty. All of these were impeachable whether committed on or off the bench as long as
they were so grave as to shame the country. Ibid.
English resigned before trial and the proceedings were
discontinued. Ibid.

11. Harold Louderback.

Louderback, a district court judge, was impeached in
1933 in five articles for "misbehavior" as a judge and
"misdemeanors" in office. The charges appeared to range
from the felonious (registering to vote at a fictitious
residence) to improprieties (such as appointing an
incompetent receiver). 76 Cong. Rec. 4914-16 (1933).
Louderback was acquitted on all charges. 6 Cannon §524.

12. Halstead L. Ritter.

Ritter, a U.S. district judge, was impeached, in 1936
for both misbehavior and high crimes and misdemeanors.
Six articles charged him with a variety of matters
including some that were criminal--willful evasion of

income tax, and practicing law while on the bench. The latter is designated by law as a "high misdemeanor." 28 U.S.C. 454. The seventh and last article charged that Ritter's offenses would prejudice the public's view of the court's fairness. It reiterated other charges mentioned. See Impeachment, Selected Materials, House Judiciary Comm. Print., 93d Cong., 1st Sess. (Oct. 1973), p. 188. Ritter was acquitted on all counts except the last.

Berger cites the Ritter case as a prime example of how the Senate has "settled" that impeachment lies for nonindictable offenses (pp. 56-58). He notes that Ritter was acquitted on individual counts, such as tax evasion, and concludes: "Thus misconduct which fell short of a specific criminal offense (for so the specific acquittals are to be understood) could yet constitute a 'high crime and misdemeanor' because it degraded the court." (p. 56). This conclusion does not derive from the record because the article on which Ritter was convicted did reiterate specific criminal charges. Moreover, the applicability of the precedent to non-judicial officers is questionable. It does not appear that Ritter argued that the charges had to be criminal to be impeachable, perhaps because some were. However, the article on which Ritter was convicted charged "misbehavior" as well as high crimes and misdemeanors, and a number of Senators filed opinions which stated that they had voted for conviction on this theory. See opinions collected in Legal Materials on Impeachment, House Judiciary Committee Print, 91st Cong., 2d Sess., (Aug. 11, 1970), pp. 284 ff. Thus, the value of this conviction in any proceeding that might be brought against an executive officer is limited. 22/

13. William O. Douglas.

The attempted impeachment of Associate Justice Douglas in 1970 is still in the minds of Congress and the public. The words of then Congressman Gerald Ford have been much quoted in recent times: "an impeachable offense is whatever a majority of the House of Representatives considers to be at a given moment in history." 116 Cong. Rec. 11912 at 11913 (1970). Certainly, if the quote is taken out of context, one can agree with Berger, who states that Ford "laid claim to an illimitable power that rings strangely in American ears" (p. 53). However, the point to which Ford was addressing himself was that the "good behavior" require-

22/ Ritter sued for his salary on the ground that the charges against him did not constitute a high crime or (continued)

- 55 -

ment shows that "a higher standard is expected of Federal judges than of any other 'civil officers' of the United States." 116 Cong. Rec. 11913. Ford was, it appears, merely expressing the frustration one faces in deriving some clear rules from past impeachments of judges.

Despite the publicity given to the Ford speech, his was not the only position taken. Counsel for Douglas filed a brief which took the narrow view of impeachable offenses:

> There is nothing in the Constitution or in the uniform practice under the Constitution to suggest that federal judges may be impeached for anything short of criminal conduct. And the prohibition against ex post facto laws, the notice requirement of due process, the protection of the First Amendment, and considerations of "separation of powers" prevent any other standard.

Memorandum on Impeachment of Federal Judges, submitted by Simon Rifkind, Counsel for Mr. Justice Douglas, reprinted in Legal Materials on Impeachment, House Committee Print, 91st Cong., 2d Sess. (Aug. 11, 1970), p. 24. Whatever the validity of the constitutional arguments, the description of the "uniform practice" regarding judges is certainly open to question, as we have seen from the accounts of impeachments of judges, supra. Cf. Berger, p. 57. It is interesting that the memoranda submitted

---

22/ (cont'd) misdemeanor. The Court of Claims held that it had no authority to review the judgment of the Senate. 84 Ct. Cl. 293, cert. denied, 300 U.S. 668 (1936).

by both Ford and Douglas ignore the two impeachments of executive officers and discuss only impeachments of judges. Legal Materials on Impeachment, supra at 6-35. This confirms to some extent the idea that the cases involving judges constitute a separate body of law from other impeachments.

A subcommittee appointed to investigate the matter described several theories concerning the grounds for impeachment of Federal judges. Assoc. Justice William O. Douglas, Final Report by the Special Subcommittee on H. Res. 920, House Judiciary Comm., 91st Cong. 2d Sess. 31-39. The report pointed out arguments by House Managers in the past that the phrase "high crimes and misdemeanors" encompassed activity not necessarily criminal (Id. at 37) and went on to state the difficulties engendered by "good behavior." The majority of the subcommittee concluded that it was not necessary for the committee to take a position on the law since the investigation had "not disclosed creditable evidence that would warrant preparation of charges on any acceptable concept of an impeachable offense." Id. at 349.

Department of Justice

FOR RELEASE AT 6:00 P.M., EDT
FRIDAY, FEBRUARY 22, 1974

THE LAW OF IMPEACHMENT

Appendix II: History of Provisions of the Constitution
Relating to Impeachment

𝕯epartment of 𝕵ustice
𝔚ashington, 𝔇.𝔒. 20530

February 21, 1974

The attached Appendices I and II, discussing
the historical background of the impeachable offense
concept are part of research on the legal aspects of
impeachment undertaken by the Office of Legal Counsel.
These are working papers.

This material is a general academic discussion,
without reference to any particular factual allegations. It does not reach conclusions or propose
solutions. It is resource material.

Robert G. Dixon, Jr.
Assistant Attorney General
Office of Legal Counsel

This material is an interim working paper prepared by the staff of the Office of Legal Counsel. The views expressed should not be regarded as an official position of the Department of Justice.

Some of the views set forth here may, as the result of further research, be subject to modification.

Robert G. Dixon, Jr.
Assistant Attorney General
Office of Legal Counsel

Table of Contents

A. The Constitutional Convention

1. Introduction

The official authorization for the Constitutional
Convention was a resolution of the Congress of the Con-
federation adopted February 21, 1787 which called for a
convention of State-appointed delegates to be held on
May 14, 1787, in Philadelphia. On that date, several
delegates appeared, but it was not until May 25 that a
sufficient number of delegates appeared to constitute
a representation of a majority of the States. On May 25,
the Convention organized and remained in continuous session
until September 17, with the exception of one adjournment
of two days over the Fourth of July and another of ten
days, from July 26 to August 6, to allow the Committee of
Detail to prepare its report.

For the first two months of its sessions the Convention
devoted itself mainly to the discussion of general principles,
modifying and developing the Randolph Resolutions presented
on behalf of Virginia. On July 23, a committee of five,
known as the Committee of Detail, was organized to prepare
and report a Constitution in conformance with the proceedings
held up until that time. The Committee members were John
Rutledge of South Carolina, Edmund Randolph of Virginia,

Nathaniel Gorham of Massachusetts, Oliver Ellsworth of Connecticut (later Chief Justice of the Supreme Court), and James Wilson of Pennsylvania. On July 24, the Committee of the Whole was discharged and the various constitutional plans referred to the Committee of Detail. On July 26, the Convention adjourned for 10 days so that the Committee of Detail could draft its report.

The Committee of Detail worked for ten days preparing a draft of the Constitution which was presented to the Convention on August 6. Records of the work of that Committee in preparing its draft have been preserved.

The August 6 draft was the subject for discussion for over one month. A Committee of Style and Revision was then formed to revise the style of and arrange the agreed upon Constitutional provisions. That Committee returned a draft on September 12, which, except for a few changes, was to become the Constitution. The final form of the Constitution was adopted on September 17.

What follows is a summary of the history of the six Constitutional clauses that specifically relate to impeachment as they were debated and modified during the Constitutional Convention. Additionally, a summary of the history

2

of three other Constitutional provisions -- rendition
(extradition), removal of judges, selection of the President --
is provided because of their relevance in interpreting the
impeachment provisions. The history of the rendition clause
contains the only specific indication of what may have been
meant by the phrase "high misdemeanor." The history of the
clauses relating to the selection of the President puts
in proper perspective many remarks made during the Constitutional Convention concerning impeachment. Virtually all
of the discussion concerning impeachment occurred during
the period when drafts of the Constitution made it applicable
only to the Chief Executive. Throughout a large part of the
Convention, it was the understanding that the executive should
be elected by the national legislature. Statements made
about impeachment on the assumption that the President was
to be elected by the national legislature might not have
been made, or might have been different, if at the time it
was realized that the President would be elected independently from the legislature. The history of the clause
concerning removal of judges is important because most
cases of impeachments have concerned the removal of judges.
Unfortunately, the history of that clause is sparse.

The source material for the history that follows is
Max Farrand's four volume work, <u>The Records of the Federal
Convention of 1787</u> (1937 Rev. Ed.) (hereinafter "Farrand").
Farrand relies principally on notes kept by James Madison
during the Constitutional Convention and a Journal of the
Convention proceedings to reconstruct the proceedings at the
Convention. The notes and records kept by other delegates
at the Convention are also used.

2. <u>Summary and Conclusions</u>

<u>What Constitutes An Impeachable Offense</u>?

Art. II, §4 of the Constitution states that treason,
bribery, or other high crimes and misdemeanors constitute
impeachable offenses. Treason is defined in the Constitution
and the elements of the crime of bribery are well-established.
The ambiguous terms are the words "high crimes and misdemeanors."
The history of Art. II, §4 tends to indicate that "high crimes
and misdemeanors" was intended to encompass some egregious
misconduct that was not criminal;<u>1</u>/ but a precise definition
of this concept is impossible.

_____

<u>1</u>/ Rules of constitutional and statutory construction may
also indicate that conclusion. Arguably, if Art. II, §4 was
intended to cover only crimes, then the word "misdemeanors"
in the phrase "high crimes and misdemeanors" would be super
fluous, assuming "high" modifies both terms. Each word in
that section should be given independent significance if such
a construction is reasonable.
      Conversely, however, the word "other" in the impeachment
clause supports a narrow "criminal" construction of "high
crimes and misdemeanors." After mentioning two crimes--treason
and bribery--the clause says: "or <u>other</u> high crimes and
misdemeanors."

No discussion of what the constitutional phrase encompassed took place in the context of impeachment at any time. The only specific discussion of the term "high misdemeanor" was in debate over rendition provisions which took place shortly before "high crimes and misdemeanors" was adopted as a justification for impeachment. In the context of debating the rendition provisions, "high misdemeanors" was rejected in favor of "other crimes" on August 28 "in order to comprehend all proper cases: it being doubtful whether 'high misdemeanor' had not a technical meaning too limited."2/ A short time later, "high crimes and misdemeanors" was substituted for "maladministration" as a justification for impeachment because that latter term was too vague.3/ Presumably, the Framers intended "high crimes and misdemeanors" to be relatively precise and not vague. Otherwise, the insertion of that phrase would not have cured the evil created by the use of "maladministration." Thus, it seems that the Framers intended the phrase "high crimes and misdemeanors" to have a relatively restricted meaning.

2/ 2 Farrand 443.

3/ 2 Farrand 550.

However, what source of law the Framers intended
to be used to define the contours of high crimes and
misdemeanors for impeachment purposes is extremely uncertain.
Comments by some of the Convention delegates tend to indicate
that the Framers had the English common law in mind. Mason
referred to the impeachment trial of Warren Hastings
in proposing that impeachment reach beyond treason and
bribery. 4/ Those offenses would not cover some of the
apparently non-criminal matters for which Hastings was
impeached. 5/ He thus moved to add "maladministration"
as a basis for impeachment, for which he later substituted
"high crimes and misdemeanors." 6/ That the Hastings
impeachment trial was referred to immediately before the
adoption of the phrase "high crimes and misdemeanors"
suggests that the Framers intended to use that term as
the British had. 7/ At one point during the Convention,
Gerry suggested the establishment of a council to advise that

---

4/ 2 Farrand 550.

5/ A Simpson, Federal Impeachment, at 167.

6/ 2 Farrand 550.

7/ However, "British practice" varied over the centuries,
and it is not at all clear that American perception went
beyond Blackstone, who stressed the narrow concept of impeachment. See Appendix I on impeachable offenses, at p. 30.

executive. 8/ He stated that such a council could be called
to account for their opinions and could be impeached, a clear
reference to impeachment against ministers advising illegal
measures upon the King in England.9/

Additionally, the statement of Hamilton in Federalist
No. 65 that the British practice was used as the model for
the federal impeachment provisions may indicate that the
Framers intended British common law, insofar as they understood it, to provide the definition of "high crimes and
misdemeanors."

However, clearly the Framers did not intend to adopt
wholesale the British practice regarding impeachment. They
rejected several aspects of that practice (e.g., no criminal
punishment, no application to private citizens). Thus, the
proper source of law to use to determine what the Framers
meant by high crimes and misdemeanors for purposes of
impeachment is uncertain.

Extremely significant is the fact that the English Parliament
could and did, in its discretion, impose a criminal penalty in
the course of impeachment. Hence, we cannot

8/ 1 Farrand 70.

9/ 4 Elliot 263.

intelligently ask the question: can American impeachments go beyond criminal "offenses," because the antecedent English practice did so? Granted the power of Parliament to impose a criminal penalty, any English impeachments could be potentially "criminal." There was thus no occasion for the English to speculate about a "crimes plus" category of impeachment, which is the insistent American question. At the same time, the American concept of impeachment, even on a "crimes plus" basis, may not encompass all crimes. The draft impeachment clause at one point contained the phrase, "against the United States." Its deletion, as a matter of style, does not change the apparent intent that only public-oriented offenses be impeachable.

Even assuming that the Framers intended to define that phrase with reference to British impeachment practice, what that practice was is very unclear. Blackstone asserted that impeachments reached only crimes.10/ He also characterized a high misdemeanor as "the mal-administration of such high officers, as are in public trust and employment" which are "usually punished by the method of parliamentary impeachment."11/

10/ 4 Blackstone 269 (Cooley 2d Ed. 1876).

11/ Id. at 121.

8

On the other hand, it appears that until after 1695, the British in fact impeached certain officers for high crimes and misdemeanors, and sometimes attached criminal penalties, when their conduct did not violate the _ordinary_ criminal law.12/ However, British practice since 1715 seems to have limited the grounds for impeachment to conventional crimes.13/ That apparent narrowing basis for impeachment is not unusual in light of the major purpose that it served in England. Initially, that purpose was to establish the doctrine of ministerial responsibility to the parliament in executing the law, the King himself being above the law.14/ By 1721, however, with parliamentary supremacy over the Crown relatively firmly established, impeachment was a dying institution.15/ Whereas 50 impeachment trials were held in Britain between 1620 and 1715, only four such trials have been held since that date.16/

Thus, it appears that the British did not have a uniform, consistent use of "high misdemeanors" in cases of impeachment. Rather, that concept changed as parliamentary government

12/ R. Berger, Impeachment: The Constitutional Problems, at 67-69.
13/ W. Holdsworth, A History of English Law, Vol. 1, p. 384 (1955 Ed.).
14/ Id. at 382-383.
15/ Id. at 384-385.
16/ Id. at 382.

replaced a royal government. Because the British had no

"Constitution," as in the United States, superior to legis-

lative enactments, the parliament needed no "Amendments"

to change, in a proper manner, its concept of high mis-

demeanors in cases of impeachment. High misdemeanor was

apparently not an immutable concept embedded in English

common law, but changed over the years in response to the

strengthening of parliamentary power over the Crown.

Because it is so uncertain whether the Framers intended

to adopt the British definition of high crimes and mis-

demeanors in cases of impeachment, and exactly what that

British definition was at any given time, the purposes of

impeachment as expressed by the Convention delegates,

the terms they rejected as a basis for impeachment, and the

Constitutional text are the most reliable guidelines to

use to determine what the Framers intended by "high crimes

and misdemeanors."

The Framers specifically rejected terms such as "mal-

administration,"17 / "neglect of duty," 18/ and "mal-

practice," 19/ to describe impeachable conduct. This

_____

17/ 2 Farrand 545.
18/ 1 Farrand 88.
19/ Id.

10

indicates that incompetence or bad performance in office was not intended to be impeachable. That conclusion, however, does not provide substantial aid regarding the extent of misconduct needed to constitute a high crime or misdemeanor. However, the purpose of the impeachment power, as gleaned from some delegate comments, indicates that an abuse of official power (e.g., to enrich oneself at the public treasury, or manipulate the organs of government to oppress the people) might constitute impeachable conduct.

At various stages of the Convention, delegates stated that impeachment was necessary to prevent a President from sparing no effort to gain reelection, [20]/ acting above the law, [21]/ or perverting his administration into a scheme of peculation or oppression [22]/ Randolph favored impeachment in part because the executive would have great opportunity to abuse his power. [23]/ Gouverneur Morris noted that impeachment would be essential to prevent executive misconduct in office [24]/ Mason, in successfully arguing that impeachment

---

[20]/ 2 Farrand 64.
[21]/ 2 Farrand 65.
[22]/ 2 Farrand 65-66.
[23]/ 2 Farrand 67.
[24]/ 2 Farrand 68-69.

should cover more than treason or bribery stated that "[a]ttempts to subvert the Constitution" should be impeachable.25/ These statements indicate that an appreciable number of delegates intended impeachment to operate as a check against gross abuse of political power.

Thus, the purpose of impeachment as expressed by some delegates at the Constitutional Convention, tends to support the conclusion that "high crimes and misdemeanors" includes an uncertain penumbra of non-criminal misconduct. On the other hand, it is equally clear from the Convention debates that only grave misconduct undermining trust in the Government was impeachable. The Framers clearly did not intend that Congress could declare any conduct impeachable; that conclusion is evidenced by the Convention's rejection of "maladministration" as a basis for impeachment because adoption of that broad term would have been tantamount to giving the executive tenure during the pleasure of two-thirds the Senate.

In addition to the foregoing essentially historical analysis, which has conflicting and inconsistent elements, a textual analysis may be instructive. Here too, some

_____
25/ 2 Farrand 550.

12

conflicting inferences can be drawn, although certain

aspects of a strictly textual analysis point in the

direction of defining "high crimes and misdemeanors" to mean

essentially criminal offenses. For this purpose the relevant

portions of the Constitution are the rendition (extradition)

clause, the sanctions clause, the pardon clause, and the jury

trial exception clause.

As already noted, the interstate rendition clause,

Art. IV, § 2, cl. 2, initially encompassed "treason, felony,

or high misdemeanor," and when the term "other crime" was

substituted for "high misdemeanor" the intent was to broaden

rather than to narrow the scope of the clause. Interstate

rendition or international extradition has always focused

on the handing over of fugitives from criminal justice.

An inference arises therefore that the delegates did not

conceive of "high misdemeanor" as having a non-criminal

content, either at the time the phrase was in the rendition

clause, or shortly thereafter when it was inserted in the

impeachment clause. On the other hand, the Convention

rejected high misdemeanors because it did not cover "proper"

cases, thereby suggesting that such a term may have included

offenses that might not be crimes and thus not properly

subject to rendition.

13

On conviction on an impeachment the sanction is removal from office, and perhaps also disqualification from future federal office, Art. I, § 3, cl. 7, but the clause goes on to preserve liability to criminal indictment after removal. This provision may suggest that the Framers thought of impeachable offenses as being primarily criminal, and wished to avoid a possible double jeopardy plea.26/

Similarly in authorizing jury trial for criminal offenses the Convention excepted cases of impeachment. Art. III, § 2, cl. 3. Impeachment also was excepted from the pardoning power, Art. II, § 2, cl. 1, which traditionally operates only in the criminal field.

Thus, the sanctions clause, the pardon clause, and the jury trial clause all suggest that the Framers had criminality very much in mind when they thought of "high crimes and misdemeanors," and they made special provision for that criminality. However, these provisions may show only that the Framers thought that impeachable offenses would be normally or frequently criminal in nature, not that impeachable offenses would be exclusively criminal

---

26/ Although the Fifth Amendment guarantee against double jeopardy was not established until after the adoption of the Constitution, that guarantee was well established in English common law long before 1787. See, Benton v. Maryland, 395 U.S. 784, 795 (1969).

The Convention's ultimate determination to place the
trial of impeachment in the Senate, rather than in a court,
might produce opposing inferences. The fact that the trier
of impeachments was changed from the Supreme Court to the
Senate on the same day that the grounds for impeachment were
broadened beyond the crimes of treason and bribery to
include "other high crimes and misdemeanors" supports the
assertion that some non-criminal conduct was impeachable.
On the other hand, the initial provision for trial by the
Supreme Court, which was in the draft until very late in
the Convention, suggests that the impeachable offense
concept initially was confined to breaches of established
law judicially cognizable.

In sum, the narrow view of the concept of "impeachable
offense" finds some textual support. The broader view finds
some support in delegate comments in the Convention, and in
the state ratification conventions, and in the hypothesis
that whatever is done is not subject to judicial review.
In such a confused situation, public opinion and political
strength may be the ultimate determiners. Perhaps the only
point on which all would agree is that _if_ the concept of
impeachable offense is a "criminal plus" concept, the plus
is centered in a gross abuse of office concept, which the
Framers did not think was tantamount to "maladministration."

3.   Grounds for Impeachment

Art. II, §4:   The President, Vice President and all Civil Officers of the United States, shall be removed from Office on Impeachment for, and Conviction of, Treason, Bribery, or other high Crimes and Misdemeanors.

On June 2, Mr. Dickinson moved that the executive be removable by the national legislature on the request of a majority of State legislatures. He did not like the plan of impeaching the Great Officers of State.

Sherman contended that the national legislature should have power to remove the executive at pleasure.

Mr. Mason stated that the fallibility of those who choose and the corruptibility of those chosen made some mode of displacing an unfit magistrate indispensable, but he objected to making the executive a legislative creature because it violated the fundamental principles of good government.

Madison and Wilson thought Dickinson's proposal would encourage intrigue in the States, and permit a minority of people to prevent the removal of a corrupt officer. Dickinson's motion lost. (1 Farrand 85-87)

The Committee of the Whole then agreed that the executive be "removable on impeachment and conviction for malpractice or neglect of duty." (1 Farrand 88)

On June 13, the Committee of the Whole reported out the Randolph Plan, as amended, which provided that the chief executive be elected by the national legislature for a

16

seven-year term and be "removable on impeachment and conviction of mal-practice or neglect of duty." (1 Farrand
226)

On June 15, the Patterson Plan was proposed which
provided for a plural executive, each removable by Congress
on application by a majority of the State Executives.
(1 Farrand 244)

On June 18, Hamilton proposed that all officers of the
United States be liable to impeachment for "mal and corrupt
conduct" and upon conviction be removed from office and
disqualified from holding any position of trust or profit.
(1 Farrand 292). The chief executive was to be popularly
elected to serve during good behavior. (Id.)

On July 19, Gouverneur Morris spoke against making the
executive too dependent on the legislature. He contended
that the President could not operate to check the legislature if that body could impeach him. (2 Farrand 53)
He discounted the danger of an unimpeachable magistrate,
noting that other high executive officials "will exercise
their functions in subordination to the Executive, and
will be amenable by impeachment to the public Justice."
(Id. at 54)

On July 20, it was agreed to make the President removable on impeachment and conviction of malpractice or neglect
of duty. (2 Farrand 61)

Pinckney and Morris moved to strike that clause, contending that the President should not be impeached while in office.

Davie and Wilson opposed that motion, arguing that if the President were not impeachable while in office he would spare no effort to gain reelection.

Morris, in support of his motion, stated that the President could do no criminal act without accomplices, who would be punished. If the President was reelected, his innocence is proven. Besides, Morris stated, who will impeach? "If impeachment is not to suspend the President's functions, mischief will continue; if suspension does result, impeachment will be nearly tantamont to displacement and will render the executive dependent on the impeaching body."

Mason argued impeachment was needed so that no man would be above the law. He noted that electors might be corrupted so that impeachment might be needed while the President was in office.

Dr. Franklin stated that impeachment would prevent the assassination of an "obnoxious" President and was the best way to punish the executive when his misconduct deserved it, and to acquit him when unjustly accused.

Morris stated that corruption and some few other offenses ought to be impeachable, but thought that the cases should be enumerated and defined.

Madison stated that some provision was needed to defend the community against the President if he became corrupt, incapacitated, or perverted his administration into a scheme of peculation or oppression. His term of office was an insufficient protection. The executive was more liable to total corruption than the legislature which consisted of many members.

Pinckney stated impeachment was unneeded and should not emanate from the legislature because it would give that body undue control over the executive.

Gerry stated that impeachment was necessary and that a good magistrate would have no fear of its use.

King stated that the impeachment provision would weaken the executive and violate Separation of Powers principles. He thought that the President should not be impeachable unless he was to hold office during good behavior like judges.

Randolph favored the impeachment provision. He thought that guilt must be punished and the executive would have great opportunity to abuse his power. He suggested that perhaps State judges should try impeachments.

Pinckney stated that the President's limited powers would make impeachment unnecessary.

Morris then changed his mind and considered impeachment necessary for cases of bribery, treachery, corruption, and incapacity. The impeachment provisions, however, should not make the executive "dependent on the Legislature."

The Convention then voted 8-1 to make the executive removable on impeachments. (See, 2 Farrand 64-69 for the entire debate.)

On July 26, the Convention agreed to make the President impeachable for "malpractice or neglect of duty." (2 Farrand 116)

In the drafts of the Committee of Detail report, the July 26 provision was initially accepted; then it was proposed that the President be removable on impeachment by the House and conviction before the Supreme Court of malpractice, neglect of duty, treason, bribery or corruption. Finally, the Committee reported on August 6 a provision that the President be impeached by the House and tried by the Supreme Court for treason, bribery or corruption. (2 Farrand 134, 145, 172, 185-186)

On August 20, Gouverneur Morris submitted a resolution that was referred to the Committee of Detail providing that the President's Council of State, consisting of the Chief Justice and the Secretaries of Commerce, Marine Affairs, State, War, and Foreign Affairs, be impeachable for neglect of duty, malversation, or corruption. (2Farrand 342-44) On August 22, a Committee of Five recommended that Judges of the Supreme Court be tried by the Senate upon impeachment by the House. (2 Farrand 367)   Neither of these proposals was adopted.

On August 27, the Convention, at the request of Morris, agreed to postpone consideration of an impeachment provision making the President removable on impeachment by the House and conviction in the Supreme Court of treason, bribery, or corruption. Morris thought that the Supreme Court was an improper tribunal to try impeachments, especially if the Chief Justice was to be part of the President's privy council. (2 Farrand 427)

On September 4, the Committee of Eleven recommended that the President be removable from office upon impeachment in the House and conviction in the Senate for treason or bribery. (2 Farrand 495) It also proposed an electoral college method of electing the President. (Id. at 493-494) In stating the reasons for an electoral college, Morris noted the "difficulty of establishing a Court of Impeachments, other than the Senate which would not be so proper for the trial nor the other branch for the impeachment of the President, if appointed by the legislature." (Id. at 500) Morris thought a conclusive reason for making the Senate instead of the Supreme Court the judge of impeachments, was that the latter was to try the President after the trial of the impeachment. (Id.)

On September 8, Mason objected to the Committee of
Eleven plan limiting impeachment to treason and bribery
because those terms would not reach many dangerous offenses,
including attempts to subvert the Constitution. For
example, he noted that Warren Hastings, under impeachment
in Britain for high crimes and misdemeanors[27] was not
guilty of treason. Because bills of attainder, which had
"saved the British Constitution," were forbidden, Mason
thought it more necessary to extend the power of impeachment.
He thus moved to make "maladministration" an impeachable
offense.

Madison objected, stating that so vague a term was
tantamount to tenure during the pleasure of the Senate.

Gouverneur Morris stated that an "election every four
years will prevent maladministration."

Mason then withdrew "maladministration" and substituted
"high crimes and misdemeanors against the State," which was
adopted by an 8-3 vote without debate.[28]   (2 Farrand 550)

Madison then objected to the Senate as a trier of Presidential impeachments. He thought such a provision made the
President too dependent on the legislature and preferred the
Supreme Court or a tribunal of which that Court would be
a part.

27/ A. Simpson, Federal Impeachment, at 167.

28/ The words "United States" were substituted for "State"
almost immediately in order to remove ambiguity. (2 Farrand
551).   22

Morris stated that the Senate was the only tribunal that would be trusted. The Supreme Court was too small and might be corrupted. He stated that "there could be no danger that the Senate would say untruly on their oaths that the President was guilty of crimes or facts, especially as in four years he can be turned out. . ."

Pinckney opposed making the Senate the trier of impeachments because it made the President too dependent upon the legislature.

Williamson stated that there was more danger of leniency than rigor towards the President by the Senate in impeachment trials, considering the number of cases in which they shared powers.

Sherman contended that the Supreme Court was an improper tribunal to try impeachments because the Justices were appointed by the President.

The Convention then voted 9-2 against the Madison proposal. (2 Farrand 551, 552)

The Convention also agreed on September 8 that the impeachment provisions should also apply to the Vice President and other civil officers of the United States. (2 Farrand 552)

The Committee of Style initially proposed that impeachable offenses be treason, bribery, or other crimes and misdemeanors against the United States. The Committee eliminated the words "against the United States" before reporting what was adopted as Art. II, §4 on September 12. (2 Farrand 575, 6(

On September 14, Rutledge and Morris moved that persons impeached be suspended from office until trial and acquittal. Madison opposed the motion on the ground that it made the President too dependent upon the legislative branch, and would give the House incentive to impeach in order temporarily to replace the President with a more favorable magistrate. Madison's position was upheld by an 8-3 vote. (2 Farrand 612)

4. Rendition (Extradition)

Art. IV, §2, cl. 2: A Person charged in any State with Treason, Felony, or other Crime, . . . shall on demand of the executive Authority of the State from which he fled, be delivered up, to be removed to the State having jurisdiction of the Crime.

As reported by the Committee of Detail, the extradition provision applied to persons charged with "treason, felony, or high misdemeanor." In the Convention on August 28, the words "high misdemeanor" were replaced by the words "other crime" in order to comprehend all proper cases; it being doubtful whether "high misdemeanor" had not a technical meaning too limited. (2 Farrand 174, 443) This change in Art. IV, §2, cl. 2 came shortly before the Convention rejected as too vague the term "maladministration" as a justification for impeachment, and substituted "high crimes and misdemeanors." From this sequence Raoul Berger draws the inference, permissible but not compelled, that the word "high" in the impeachment clause, Art. II, §4, modifies both "crimes" and "misdemeanors". Impeachment: The Constitutional Problems, at 74 and n. 108 thereon. He contends that these changes exhibit an intent by the Convention to embrace the limited, technical meaning of high crimes and misdemeanors at common law for purposes of impeachment. See, Impeachment: The Constitutional Problems, at 86-87.

25

Additionally, Charles Pinckney, a delegate from
South Carolina, referred to "high misdemeanor" as a
crime in connection with discussing the rendition
clause in a pamphlet he published shortly after the
Constitutional Convention adjourned. (3 Farrand 112)

5. Grounds for Removal of Judges

Art. III, § 1: The Judges, both of the supreme and inferior courts, shall hold their Offices during good Behavior . . . .

The Randolph Resolutions introduced on May 29 provided that federal judges should hold offices during good behavior. (1 Farrand 23) The "good behavior" standard of tenure was not opposed until August 27 when Dickinson moved to permit federal judges to be removed by the executive on application by the Senate and House. (1 Farrand 116, 226, 244, 292; 2 Farrand 44, 132, 146, 172, 186, 428) Opposing Dickinson's motion, Morris stated that it was a contradiction to say judges would hold office during good behavior yet be removable without a trial. Moreover, it was fundamentally wrong to subject judges to so arbitrary an authority.

Sherman saw no contradiction in Dickinson's proposal and stated that British statutes contained a like provision.

Wilson contended that judges would be in a bad situation if their tenure were to depend on every gust of faction prevailing in the two branches of the legis-

27

lature. He thought British statutes created less danger
to judicial independence because the Lords and Commons
were less likely to agree than the House and Senate.

Randolph opposed Dickinson's proposal because it
would weaken judicial independence too much.

Dickinson thought that the House and Senate would
not unite for improper reasons.

Dickinson's proposal lost 7-1 (see, 2 Farrand 428-
429 for the entire debate).

On September 12, the Committee of Style reported
out that part of Art. III, § 1 giving federal judges
tenure "during good behavior." This provision was
adopted without further discussion. (2 Farrand 600)

In respect to enforcement, it is uncertain whether
the delegates viewed the "good behavior" provision as
the basis for some kind of trial, as Morris inferred,
or as an added ground for judicial impeachment.

6. Impeachment Power of the House of Representatives

Art. I, §2, cl. 5: The House of Representatives . . . shall have the sole Power of Impeachment.

The proposal to give the House the sole power to impeach appeared on May 29 in a plan proposed by Charles Pinckney. (3 Farrand 600) That plan was not debated but was referred to the Committee of Detail. A draft of the Committee of Detail report and its final report referred to the Convention on August 6 gave the House the sole power to impeach. (2 Farrand 136, 178-179) Before this time, no other proposals had specifically given any official body the power to impeach. In one Committee of Detail draft, the House of Representatives was characterized as the "grand Inquest of the Nation" in authorizing its impeachment power. (2 Farrand 164) If that language had been accepted for the Constitution it would aid the argument for a broad view of impeachable offenses; its absence inferentially supports the narrower view derived from the constitutional text.

On August 9, the Convention adopted the provision giving the House the sole power to impeach without debate or dissent. (2 Farrand 231) The Committee of Style made no changes in the clause, (2 Farrand 566, 591), which was subsequently adopted in approving the Constitution.

29

7. Senate Trial of Impeachments

Art. I, § 3, cl. 6: The Senate shall have the sole Power to try all Impeachments. When sitting for that Purpose, they shall be on Oath or Affirmation. When the President of the United States is tried, the Chief Justice shall preside: And no Person shall be convicted without the Concurrence of two thirds of the Members present.

On May 29, the Randolph Resolutions were submitted to the Convention proposing that inferior national tribunals try and the Supreme Court hear and determine in the "dernier" resort "impeachments of any National officers." The national executive was to be elected by the legislature for an unspecified term and to be ineligible for reelection. (1 Farrand 21-22) On that same day, Charles Pinckney of South Carolina proposed a plan of government lodging the power to impeach the President in the "house of Delegates" for "Treason bribery or Corruption" with trial in the "Supreme Court." (3 Farrand 600) [29]

On May 30, the Convention resolved itself into a Committee of the Whole to discuss the Randolph plan point by point. (1 Farrand 29)

On June 1, in discussing the executive article of the Randolph Plan, Mr. Bedford of Delaware opposed a 7-year executive term because a chief executive might prove incapable

---

[29] A reconstructed version of the Pinckney plan prepared by certain scholars provides for impeachment by the House of all United States officers for "all Crimes . . . in their Offices" and trial by Senators and Judges of the Federal Court. (3 Farrand 601-608)

of discharging his duties. "An impeachment . . . would be no cure for this evil, as an impeachment would reach misfeasance only, not incapacity." (1 Farrand 68-69)

Randolph desired a plural executive, in part because a single executive could not be impeached until the expiration of his term, or else he would be too dependent on the legislature, contrary to "the fixed Genius of America . . ." (1 Farrand 71)

Gerry of Massachusetts desired an executive council whose opinions would be recorded and who could be impeached for those opinions. (1 Farrand 70)

On June 13, the Committee of the Whole adopted a resolution extending the jurisdiction of the national judiciary to "impeachments of any national officers . . ." (1 Farrand 224, 231)

On June 15, William Patterson of New Jersey presented his "New Jersey Plan" calling for a unicameral legislature, a plural executive elected by Congress, and a Supreme Court. The Supreme Court was to try impeachments of federal officers. (1 Farrand 244).

On June 18, Alexander Hamilton proposed a plan in which the chief executive and senators were to serve during good behavior. (1 Farrand 291-292) The chief executive, senators and "all officers of the United States" could be impeached for "mal- and corrupt conduct" and tried by a court whose composition is uncertain. (1 Farrand 292) One copy of that plan proposed that the trial court consist of Supreme Court justices

plus the senior judge of each State, and another copy
confined the court to state judges. (3 Farrand 618-619)

On June 19, the Committee of the Whole in effect put
aside the New Jersey Plan and voted to give preference to
the Randolph Resolutions. (1 Farrand 312, 322)

On July 18, during debate on the method of appointing
judges, Mr. Mason stated that the manner of appointment
would depend in some degree on the manner of trying executive
impeachments. If the judges were to try the executive, they
ought not be appointed by him. (2 Farrand 41-42) Gouverneur
Morris stated that judges should not try executive impeachments
because they would be drawn into legislative intrigues and an
impartial trial frustrated. (2 Farrand 42) At some point during
the debate, it was unanimously agreed to remove from the national
judiciary jurisdiction over "impeachments of national Officers."
(2 Farrand 39)

In an early draft of the report of the Committee of Detail,
impeachments were to be tried before the Senate and federal judges.
(2 Farrand 136) In later drafts, the supreme judiciary was given
authority to try impeachments. (2 Farrand 145, 157). A subsequent draft again placed the authority to try impeachments with
the Senate and judges of the federal court. (2 Farrand 159)
A final draft extended the original jurisdiction of the Supreme
Court to the trial of "Impeachments of Officers of the United
States." (2 Farrand 172-173) That provision was included in the
Committee of Detail plan reported to the Convention on August 6.
(2 Farrand 186)

On August 22, a Committee of Five headed by Mr. Rutledge made several proposals including one that Supreme Court judges be tried by the Senate upon impeachment by the House. (2 Farrand 367) That proposal was never voted upon.

On August 27, the Convention rejected by a 7-1 vote a motion to make federal judges removable by the executive on the application by the Senate and House. (2 Farrand 423)

On September 4, a Committee of Eleven proposed that the Senate have the sole power to try impeachments, with a two-thirds vote of Members present needed for conviction. (2 Farrand 493) That Committee also proposed an electoral college method of electing the President. (2 Farrand 493-494) In favoring the electoral college method of electing the Presi-dent, Morris noted the difficulty of establishing a court of impeachments, other than the Senate; that latter body would be inappropriate to try and the House would be inappropriate to impeach the President if those bodies appointed him. (2 Farrand 500) In the trial of Presidential impeachments, the Committee proposed that the Chief Justice preside, (2 Farrand 498), which was agreed to on September 7. (2 Farrand 532)

On September 8, the Convention agreed that the Senate have authority to try "all impeachments: but no person shall be convicted without the concurrence of two-thirds of the Members present; and every Member shall be on oath." (2 Farrand 547) On the same date, the Vice President and

33

other civil officers of the United States were made subject to impeachment in the same manner as the President. (2 Farrand 552)

On September 10, Randolph objected to several provisions in the proposed Constitution, one of which was the Senate's power to try an impeachment of the executive. (2 Farrand 563) He proposed a resolution to recommend that State ratification conventions have power to adopt, reject, or amend the proposed Constitution, with a subsequent Convention having power to act on proposed State alterations. That proposal was tabled. (2 Farrand 563-564)

The Committee of Style drafted what in substance became Art. I, § 3, cl. 6 in two separate sections. (2 Farrand 572, 574) It reported on September 12 a provision that ultimately became Art. I, § 3, cl. 6 except for the failure to provide that Senators be on oath or affirmation when trying impeachments. (2 Farrand 595) The final form of that clause was agreed to on September 14, (2 Farrand 610). On that same date, the Convention rejected by a vote of 8-3 a motion of Rutledge and Morris to suspend officers who are impeached until they be tried and acquitted. Madison argued, in opposition to that motion, that the impeachment provisions already made the President too dependent upon the legislative branch, and that the proposal would put the President under the power of the House, which might at any moment impeach the President to make way temporarily for a more favorable magistrate.

(2 Farrand 612-13)

8. Sanctions

Art. I, § 3, cl. 7: Judgment in Cases of Impeachment shall not extend further than to removal from Office, and disqualification to hold and enjoy any Office of honor, Trust or Profit under the United States: but the Party convicted shall nevertheless be liable and subject to indictment, Trial, Judgment and Punishment, according to law.

This clause originated in the Committee of Detail and was reported out in final from on August 6, and was adopted without debate. (2 Farrand 173, 187, 438) The Committee of Style left the clause unchanged, and it was agreed to by the Convention. (2 Farrand 576, 648)

9. Inapplicability of Pardon Power

Art. II, §2, cl. 1: The President . . . shall have power to Grant Reprieves and Pardon for Offenses against the United States, except in Cases of Impeachment.

On June 18, Hamilton proposed that the President have the power to pardon all "offenses except treason; which he shall not pardon without the approval of the Senate." (1 Farrand 292) The Committee of Detail drafts and its report to the Convention on August 6 proposed that the President's pardoning power be limited only so not impleadable as a defense to an impeachment. (2 Farrand 146, 171, 185) (That proposal was modelled after the English Act of Settlement (1700) which foreclosed the defense of pardon to an impeachment, but gave the King power to pardon after conviction. See, R. Berger, Impeachment: The Constitutional Problems, at 84-85.) However, in England criminal penalties could be imposed by impeachment, and private persons were also subject to impeachment -- features lacking in the American provisions.

On August 25, it was agreed to remove the President's power to pardon in cases of impeachment. A motion to substitute the clause "but his pardon shall not be pleadable in bar" in cases of impeachment was rejected. (2 Farrand 411, 419) That wholesale removal of the President's pardon power in cases of impeachment remained the same throughout the remainder of the Convention without debate. (2 Farrand 575, 599, 648) The President therefore may not remove a disqualification to hold future office, but could pardon a person convicted under a post-impeachment indictment.

10. Inapplicability of Jury Trial

Art. III, §2, cl. 3: The Trial of all Crimes, except in Cases of Impeachment, shall be by Jury. . . .

On August 6, the Committee of Detail reported out a provision requiring a jury trial for all criminal offenses, except in cases of impeachment. (2 Farrand 187) On August 27, Mason also proposed that all crimes, except in cases of impeachment, be by jury. (2 Farrand 433) On August 28, this provision was adopted (2 Farrand 434, 438), and became part of Art. III, §2, cl. 3, without further debate. (2 Farrand 576, 601) During this period of the Convention it was still contemplated that the Supreme Court would try impeachments, so a jury would have been theoretically feasible, absent this exception provision. This contemplation of jury trial supports an inference that the delegate's conceived impeachable offenses to be criminal in nature.

11. Selection of the President

Art. II, §1, cl. 1-4: [Clauses 1-4]. Each State shall appoint, in such Manner as the Legislature thereof may direct, a Number of Electors, equal to the whole number of Senators and Representatives to which the State may be entitled in the Congress: but no Senator or Representative, or Person holding an Office of Trust or Profit under the United States, shall be appointed an Elector.

The Electors shall meet in their respective States, and vote by Ballot for two Persons, of whom one at least shall not be an Inhabitant of the same State with themselves. . . . The Person having the greatest Number of Votes shall be the President, if such Number be a Majority of the whole Number of Electors appointed; . . . and if no Person have a Majority, then from the five highest on the List the said House shall in like Manner chuse the President. But in chusing the President, the Votes shall be taken by States, the Representation from each State having one Vote; . . . . In every Case, after the Choice of the President, the Person having the greatest Number of Votes of the Electors shall be the Vice President. . . . (Prior to Twelfth Amendment.)

Summary

Although the history of the clauses relating to the selection of the President is lengthy, that history essentially reveals the following. Several Convention delegates who desired a strong legislature wanted the President to be selected by that body. Other delegates, including Madison and Hamilton, preferred a vigorous executive that could operate as a check against legislative excesses. The latter delegates wanted Presidential selection by a body other than the national legislature and their preference ultimately prevailed.

Proceedings at the Constitutional Convention

The Randolph Resolutions introduced on May 29 provided for a national executive to be chosen by the national legis-

40

lature for an unspecified term of years.   (1 Farrand 21)

On June 1, the duration of the executive term and the mode of his appointment were debated as follows:

> "Mr. Wilson said he was almost unwilling to declare the mode which he wished to take place, being apprehensive that it might appear chimerical. He would say however at least that in theory he was for an election by the people; Experience, particularly in N. York and Massts, shewed that an election of the first magistrate by the people at large, was both a convenient and successful mode. The objects of choice in such cases must be persons whose merits have general notoriety.

> Mr. Sherman was for the appointment by the Legislature, and for Making him absolutely dependent on that body, as it was the will of that which was to be executed. An independence of the Executive on the supreme Legislative, was in his opinion the very essence of tyranny if there was any such thing.

> Mr. Wilson moves that the blank for the term of duration should be filled with three years, observing at the same time that he preferred this short period, on the supposition that a re-eligibility would be provided for.

> Mr. Pinkney moves for seven years.

> Mr. Sherman was for three years, and agst. the doctrine of rotation as throwing out of office the men best qualified to execute its duties.

> Mr. Mason was for seven years at least, and for prohibiting a re-eligibility as the best expedient both for preventing the effect of a false complaisance on the side of the Legislature towards unfit characters, and a temptation on the side of the Executive to intrigue with the Legislature for a re-appointment.

> Mr. Bedford was strongly opposed to so long a term as seven years. He begged the committee to consider what the situation of the Country would be, in case the first magistrate should be saddled on it for such period and it should be found on trial that he did not possess the qualifications ascribed to him, or should lose them after his appointment. An impeachment he said

41

would be no cure for this evil, as an impeachment would reach misfeasance only, not incapacity. He was for a triennial election, and for an ineligibility after a period of nine years."

By a 5-4 vote, the Committee of the Whole then agreed to an Executive term of seven years. (See, 1 Farrand 68-69 for the debate)

The mode of appointing the executive was the next question.

Mr. Wilson renewed his declarations in favor of an appointment by the people. He wished to derive not only both branches of the legislature from the people, without the intervention of the State legislature, but the executive also in order to make them as independent as possible of each other, as well as of the States. It was agreed to postpone consideration of that issue. (1 Farrand 69)

Also on June 1, Randolph expressed favor for a plural executive because a single executive, if impeachable before expiration of his office, would be too dependent on the legislature. (1 Farrand 71)

Madison observed either on June 1 or 2, that to prevent a man from holding an office longer than he ought, he may for malpractice be impeached and removed. (1 Farrand 74)

On June 2, the Committee of the Whole rejected by a 7-2 vote Wilson's proposal that in substance provided for the selection of the President by electors representing State districts elected by the people.

Mr. Gerry opposed election of the executive by the national legislature. He thought that it would create intrigue and corruption in the legislature. However, he opposed any direct election of electors as Wilson proposed because the people were too ignorant and liable to deception. (1 Farrand 80)

It was then agreed that the executive should be chosen by the national legislature for a seven-year term. (Id.)

On June 9, Gerry proposed that the national executive be elected by the state executives. An appointment by the national legislature would not give the executive sufficient independence. Gerry's motion lost 9-0. (1 Farrand 175-176)

On June 13, the Committee of the Whole reported out the Randolph Plan, as amended, providing a seven-year term for a single national executive to be chosen by the national legislature. (1 Farrand 226)

On June 15, William Patterson presented his New Jersey Plan providing for a unicameral legislature (with each state having one vote) and a plural executive elected by Congress. (1 Farrand 243-244)

On June 18, Hamilton sketched a plan of government in which an executive would be chosen to serve during good behavior by electors elected by the people in State districts. (1 Farrand 292)

On July 17, the Convention reconsidered the provision providing that the executive be chosen by the national legislature.

Gouverneur Morris opposed the provision stating that the executive would be the creature of the legislature if appointed and impeachable by that body. Legislative selection would promote intrigue and faction. He favored electing the President by the people at large. (2 Farrand 29)

Mr. Sherman thought that the sense of the nation would be better expressed by the legislature, than by the people at large. (Id.)

Wilson, favoring the election of the President by the people, thought that the executive if selected by the legislature would be too dependent on that body to stand between its intrigues and the liberty of the people. (2 Farrand 30).

Mr. Pinckney opposed an election by the people because they would be led by a few active and designing men. He thought that the national legislature, most immediately interested in the laws made by themselves, would be most attentive to the choice of a fit man to execute them. (Id.)

Gouverneur Morris thought the people intelligent enough to elect the President. He thought that an executive chosen by the national legislature would not be independent and thus tyranny by the legislature would result. (2 Farrand 31)

Mason opposed election of the President by the people because they did not have the requisite capacity to judge the merits of the candidates. (Id.)

By a 9-1 vote, the Convention rejected the proposal to make the executive elected by the people instead of the legislature. Immediately thereafter it rejected a motion that the executive be chosen by electors appointed by individual State legislatures, and agreed that he be chosen by the national legislature. (2 Farrand 32)

The propriety of a 7-year term for the executive was then debated. Mr. Brown preferred a shorter term since the executive was eligible for re-election. (2 Farrand 33)

Dr. McClurg moved to have the President serve during good behavior to make him independent of the legislature. He conceived the independence of the executive to be equally essential as the independence of the judiciary department. (Id.)

Gouverneur Morris seconded and supported McClurg's motion. (Id.)

Madison generally supported McClurg's motion. He objected to making the executive dependent on the legislature by having that branch control his election. He thought those two branches must be distinct and independent in a well constituted Republic so that the legislature could not exercise tyrannical power. Whether the plan proposed

45

was a proper one for establishing executive independence depended upon the practicability of instituting an adequate impeachment tribunal. (2 Farrand 35)

Mason opposed the motion, stating that it would lead to monarchy. He added that it would be impossible adequately to define misbehavior, and perhaps impossible to compel so high an offender to submit to trial. (Id.)

Madison was not apprehensive of any steps towards monarchy and thought legislatures were most in need of restraint. (Id.)

The Convention then rejected the motion to make the executive's term during good behavior and a motion to strike seven years as the duration. (2 Farrand 36)

On July 19, Ellsworth moved to make the President elected by electors appointed by State legislatures and allocated according to State population. (2 Farrand 57)

Rutledge opposed all modes of appointment except by the national legislature. (Id.)

A proposal to have the national executive selected by electors chosen by the national legislature lost; but a proposal to have the executive elected by electors chosen by the State legislatures succeeded. (2 Farrand 58)

The Convention then agreed to keep the executive eligible for a second term. (Id.) On the question of his term of office, seven years was rejected and six years adopted.

Gouverneur Morris favored a short term, in order to
avoid impeachments, which would otherwise be necessary. (Id.)

Mr. Butler was against frequent elections because
Georgia and South Carolina were too distant to send electors
often. (Id.)

Ellsworth was for a six-year term. Frequent elections
would not give the executive sufficient independence. He
observed that there "must be duties which will make him
unpopular for the moment. There will be outs as well as ins.
His administration therefore will be attacked and misrepre-
sented." (Id.)

On July 24, the Convention reconsidered the mode of
electing the President. Mr. Houston moved that he be appointed
by the national legislature instead of by electors appointed
by the State legislatures. He feared that capable men would
not undertake the service of electors from the more distant
States. (2 Farrand 99)

Gerry opposed the motion and thought Houston's fear
unwarranted. If the President was to be elected by the
national legislature, he would have to be ineligible a
second time to maintain his independence, an ineligibility
he disliked. (2 Farrand 100)

Mr. Strong saw no necessity in making a legislatively-
elected President ineligible for a second term because new
legislative elections would intervene and free the President's
second appointment from the same set of men who first appointed
him. He did not think that gratitude for the President's

past appointment would produce the same effect as dependence for his future appointment, but if true, the same objection could be lodged against the President's dependence upon Presidential electors. (Id.)

Mr. Williamson favored a seven-year term for an executive to be chosen by the national legislature and to be ineligible for a second term. He also preferred a plural executive because a single magistrate would feel the spirit of a King. (Id., 2 Farrand 101)

Mr. Houston's motion that the executive be appointed by the national legislature was adopted by a 7-4 vote. (Id.)

Luther Martin and Gerry then moved to make the executive ineligible for a second term. (Id.)

Ellsworth opposed the motion stating that a worthy executive should be re-elected. (Id.)

Gerry thought the executive should be independent of the legislature and that a long term -- 10, 15 or even 20 -- years would secure that independence with ineligibility afterwards. (2 Farrand 102)

Mr. King was for re-eligibility. He thought it too great an advantage to give up for the small effect it would have on the executive's dependence on the legislature if impeachments are to lie, which in effect would render the executive's tenure during legislative pleasure. (Id.)

Motions were then made to make the executive's term
8, 11, 15, and 20 years. (Id.)

Wilson thought all these motions sprang from a defective
mode of electing the executive and trying to rid the executive
from too much dependence on the legislature. (Id.) He then
proposed a six-year term for an executive to be chosen by a
small number from the national legislature who would be in
turn chosen by lot. This mode would decrease intrigue and
executive dependence on the legislature. (2 Farrand 103)

Gouverneur Morris thought a legislatively-elected executive
the worst mode of appointment. "Such appointment power coupled
with the impeaching power would make the executive a legislative
creature. He had been opposed to the impeachment, but was
now convinced that impeachments must be provided for, if the
executive appointment was to be of any duration. No man
would say, that an executive known to be in the pay of an
Enemy, should not be removable in some way or other." He
believed that a too weak executive would lead to legislative
usurpation of his powers and a too strong executive would
usurp legislative powers. He admitted the difficulty in striking
the right balance, and preferred a short term, a re-eligibility,
and a mode of electing the President different than by the
national legislature. (2 Farrand 103-105)

Consideration of a motion to adopt Wilson's plan for
electing the President by electors taken by lot from the

national legislature was postponed.   (2 Farrand 106)

On July 25, a motion by Ellsworth to make the President elected by Congress for his first term, but by electors chosen by State legislatures if he ran for re-election was defeated 7-4.   (2 Farrand 111)

Ellsworth thought his plan a means of permitting the re-election of a deserving magistrate without making him dependent on the legislature.   (2 Farrand 109)

Gerry opposed an election of the executive by the legislature and moved that the executive be appointed by the Governors and Presidents of the States, with the advice of their Councils, and if no Councils exist by electors chosen by the State legislatures.   (Id.)

Madison opposed any legislatively-elected executive because (1) the latter would be too dependent on the former; (2) that mode of election would divide the legislature and promote intrigue; (3) the candidate would probably render his administration subservient to the views of the faction to whom he owed his election; and (4) foreign powers would mix their intrigues in the election. He desired the President to be elected by the people at large.   (2 Farrand 109-111)

Pinckney's motion providing that no person shall serve in the executive more than 6 years in 12 years was defeated 6-5. (2 Farrand 115) During the debate on that motion, Gouverneur Morris stated that three evils to be guarded against in determining the mode of electing the executive were (1) undue influence of the legislature; (2) instability in the executive

50

and (3) misconduct in office. As to the latter evil, he noted impeachments would be essential and hence an additional reason against an election by the legislature. (2 Farrand 112-113)

On July 26, the Convention adopted by a 7-3 vote a motion providing a seven-year term for the executive to be chosen by the national legislature and to be ineligible for a second term. (2 Farrand 120) This mode of election was reported out of the Committee of Detail to the Convention on August 6. (2 Farrand 185)

On August 24, the Convention rejected several motions to make the President elected by the people. (2 Farrand 402, 404)

On September 4, the Committee of Eleven proposed that the President be chosen by electors appointed by State legislatures. (2 Farrand 493-494) Gouverneur Morris stated the following reasons in favor of the plan:

> The 1st. was the danger of intrigue and faction
> if the appointment should be made by the Legislature.
> 2. the inconveniency of an ineligibility required by
> that mode in order to lessen its evils. 3. The
> difficulty of establishing a Court of Impeachments,
> other than the Senate which would not be so proper
> for the trial nor the other branch for the impeach-
> ment of the President, if appointed by the Legislature.
> 4. No body had appeared to be satisfied with an appoint-
> ment by the Legislature. 5. Many were anxious even for
> an immediate choice by the people-- 6-- the indispensable
> necessity of making the Executive independent of the
> Legislature. -- As the Electors would vote at the same time
> throughout the U.S. and at so great a distance from each
> other, the great evil of cabal was avoided. It would be
> impossible also to corrupt them. A conclusive reason for
> making the Senate instead of the Supreme Court the Judge of
> impeachments, was that the latter was to try the President
> after the trial of the impeachment. (2 Farrand 500)

51

Pinckney o' ected to the plan of the Committee of Eleven for the following reasons:

> 1. That it threw the whole appointment in fact into the hands of the Senate. 2-- The Electors will be strangers to the several candidates and of course unable to decide on their comparative merits. 3. It makes the Executive reeligible which will endanger the publi liberty. 4. It makes the same body of men which will in fact elect the President his Judges in case of an impeachment. (2 Farrand 501)

No action was taken on the Committee of Eleven proposal at that time. (2 Farrand 502) Rutledge opposed the plan and successfully moved that the Convention take up the proposal for a seven-year term for an executive to be elected by the national legislature and to be ineligible for reelection. (2 Farrand 511-515)

The Committee of Eleven plan of the electoral college method of electing the President was reconsidered on September 6. (2 Farrand 521)

Wilson opposed the plan as throwing too much power to the Senate (The Senate was to choose the President from the five highest vote-getters if none had a majority):

> They will have in fact, the appointment of the President, and through his dependence on them, the virtual appointment to offices; among others the offices of the Judiciary Department. They are to make Treaties; and they are to try all impeachments. In allowing them thus to make the Executive & Judiciary appointments, to be the Court of impeachments, and to make Treaties which are to be laws of the land, the Legislative, Executive & Judiciary powers are all blended in one branch of the Government. (2 Farrand 522-523)

Hamilton favored the electoral college method of electing the President rather than the Committee of Detail plan, which he characterized as creating the greatest opportunities and motives for corruption. (2 Farrand 524-525)

Motions to make the President's term 7 or 6 years instead of 4 years failed. (2 Farrand 525), and it was agreed to make the President chosen by electors appointed by State legislatures. (Id, 2 Farrand 528)

The Committee of Style reported to the Convention on September 12 the electoral college method of electing the President, (2 Farrand 597), which was adopted without further debate.

B.   State Ratification Conventions

This section contains three parts. First, a summary of the proceedings at the State ratification conventions concerning impeachment and conclusions therefrom. Second, indexes of statements made concerning grounds for impeachment and checks upon the powers of Congress. Third, a more complete compilation of the statements at the State ratification conventions relevant to limiting power and abuse of office with special reference to impeachment.

1.   Introduction and Summary

The State ratification debates, with the exception of Virginia, New York, and North Carolina, were badly or very incompletely reported. In three States - Delaware, New Jersey, and Georgia - the convention proceedings were not reported at all.[30]   Because of the incomplete reporting of the State conventions, it is difficult, on the basis of the existing reports, to draw firm conclusions regarding the meaning of the constitutional provisions.

In 1836, Jonathan Elliot published the most thorough compilation of the proceedings at the State ratification conventions that exists today. Other than a few references to Farrand, Elliot is the source for all references to the State ratification debates.

30/   See, J. Goebel, <u>History of the Supreme Court of the United States</u>, Vol. 1, p. 324. (1971).

Impeachable Offenses

A number of statements made during the ratification debates indicate that serious abuse and manipulation of power, even though not rising to the level of criminal conduct, was thought to be impeachable conduct. Many of the remarks about impeachment of the President and civil officers at the state ratifying conventions were made in general terms without specific contemplation of the Presidency. It is clear also that some delegates contemplated impeachment as a check on Congress and especially the Senate, and feared the Senate would not convict its own. [31/]

Several convention delegates stated that the purpose of impeachment was to prevent abuse of power. [32/] The following kinds of conduct are representative of examples of conduct by the President, Senate, or other officers which some delegates described as constituting

---

[31/] The Senator William Blount precedent of 1798 does seem to have determined that the Senate will not try its members on an impeachment. For discussion see Appendix I.

[32/] See, e.g., 2 J. Elliot, The Debates in the several State Conventions on the adoption of the Federal Constitution (1836) 85-86, 168-169, 480 (hereinafter referred to as "Elliot").

impeachable offenses: malconduct, [33/] making bad treaties, [34/] bad advice, [35/] abuse of power, [36/] betrayal of
public trust, [37/] misconduct, [38/] great offenses, [39/] high
crimes and misdemeanors against the government, [40/] acts
of great injury to the community, [41/] acting from some
corrupt motive, [42/] giving false information to the
Senate [43/] pardoning a suspicious man with whom the
President was connected, [44/] and the President's failure

33/   2 Elliot 168-169

34/   2 Elliot 477, 4 Elliot 124-125, 268, 3 Elliot 512.

35/   4 Elliot 263.

36/   2 Elliot 85-86, 168-169, 4 Elliot 114, 276,
3 Elliot 516.

37/   4 Elliot 126-128, 281.

38/   4 Elliot 32, 3 Elliot 201.

39/   2 Elliot 11, 4 Elliot 34.

40/   4 Elliot 113-114.

41/   Id.

42/   4 Elliot 126-128.

43/   Id.

44/   3 Elliot 498, 500.

to call all Senators to ratify a treaty. [45/] The examples indicate that for a number of delegates criminal conduct was not a prerequisite for impeachment. Additionally, several delegates clearly distinguished between impeachable conduct and criminal conduct and noted that each type has its distinct punishment. [46/]

45/ Id. at 516.

46/ See, e.g., 2 Elliot 538, 4 Elliot 37, 44-45, 47, 48, 113-114.

Judicial Review

Several statements made during the state conventions lend support to the conclusion that no judicial review was contemplated. It was recognized by various State delegates that giving the Senate power to try impeachments blended the legislative and judicial powers in one body contrary to the general theory behind the allocation of powers under the Constitution.[47] The possibility that the Senate would abuse its impeachment power was specifically considered.[48] However, the checks upon such abuse mentioned by delegates were the two-thirds vote needed for conviction,[49] the presence of the Chief Justice,[50] the prerequisite of House impeachment,[51] the fact that the Senators would be under oath,[52] and

---

47/ 2 Elliot 476-477, 504-505, 530, 534-535, 4 Elliot 121, 129.

48/ 2 Elliot 323, 476-477, 478, 504-505.

49/ 4 Elliot 44-45, 47.

50/ Id.

51/ 2 Elliot 323, 504-505.

52/ 4 Elliot 44-45, 47.

the general electorate.[53/] Nowhere is judicial review mentioned as a check. Yet, in several of the conventions, delegates mentioned judicial review as a check against unconstitutional legislation.[54/] It thus seems unlikely that having in mind both the concept of judicial review and the potential abuse of the power to try impeachments by the Senate, State convention delegates would have failed to specify judicial review as a check against "improper" impeachments if such review had been intended.

James Iredell, at the North Carolina Convention, stated that the Senate was made the trier of impeachments because an inferior tribunal, including the Supreme Court in their view, might be too awed by so powerful an accuser, i.e., the House of Representatives.[55/] That awe would exist whether or not that inferior

---

53/ 2 Elliot 504-505, 4 Elliot 161-162, 171-172.

54/ 2 Elliot 196, 445-446, 3 Elliot 553.

55/ 4 Elliot 113-114.

tribunal exercised original or appellate jurisdiction, thus suggesting that the courts were not to exercise judicial review in cases of impeachment.

The fact that delegates to the Constitutional Convention and State ratification conventions expressed the view that Congress was to exercise only enumerated powers does not require the inference that judicial review of impeachments and convictions was intended. That mode of reasoning begs the crucial question of whether the unfettered power to determine what conduct is impeachable was given to Congress. [56]

---

[56] Art. I, § 2, cl. 5 gives the House of Representatives the "sole" power of impeachment. Art. I, § 3, cl. 6 gives the Senate the "sole" power to try impeachments.

2. <u>Index of Statements Made By Delegates In State Ratification Conventions Regarding Grounds for Impeachment and Checks Upon Congress</u>

<u>Grounds for Impeachment</u>

The following is a compilation and paraphrase of statements made at State ratification conventions describing what type of conduct would be impeachable.

<u>Massachusetts Convention:</u>

1. Mr. Ames: Impeachment lies only against "great offenders." (2 Elliot 11)

2. General Brooks: Conduct exciting "suspicion." (2 Elliot 5)

3. Mr. Bowdoin: Abuse of Power. (2 Elliot 75-86)

4. Mr. Stillman: Malconduct and abuse of power. (2 Elliot 168-169)

Pennsylvania Convention:

  1. James Wilson (a leading delegate at the Constitu-
      tional Convention): Making bad treaties. (2 Elliot
      477)

South Carolina Convention:

  1. Judge Pendleton: Giving bad advice (4 Elliot 263)

  2. John Rutledge (a delegate at the Constitutional
      Convention): Making a bad treaty. (4 Elliot 268)

  3. Edward Rutledge: Abuse of trust. (4 Elliot 276)

  4. General Charles Pinckney (a delegate to the
      Constitutional Convention): Betrayal of trust.
      (4 Elliot 281)

North Carolina Convention:

  1. James Iredell: Misconduct, misdemeanor in office
      high crime and misdemeanor against the government,
      acts of great injury to the community, acting to
      prejudice the people, abuse of trust, error of
      the heart, receiving a bribe or acting from a
      corrupt motive, giving false information to the
      Senate, corruption or acting for some wicked
      motive. (4 Elliot 32, 109-110, 113-114, 126-128)

  2. Mr. Maclaine: Great offenses: high crimes and
      misdemeanors, misdemeanors, and maladministration.
      (4 Elliot 34, 44-45, 47)

3. Governor Johnston: High crimes and misdemeanors in public office. (4 Elliot 48)

4. Mr. Spaight: Abuse of trust; making a bad treaty. (4 Elliot 114, 124)

5. Mr. Spencer: Misdemeanor in office; making a bad treaty. (4 Elliot 116-118, 124-125)

Virginia Convention:

1. Mr. Nicholas: Maladministration (3 Elliot 17)

2. Governor Randolph: Misbehavior, dishonesty, receiving foreign emoluments. (3 Elliot 201, 368, 486)

3. Mr. Mason: Making a treaty after being bribed. (3 Elliot 486)

4. James Madison (a leading delegate at the Constitutional Convention): Pardoning a criminal with whom the President was in collusion; summoning only a few Senators to approve a treaty; abuse of power. (3 Elliot 498, 500, 516)

5. Patrick Henry (a delegate at the Constitutional Convention): Making bad treaties; the minister who would sacrifice the interest of the nation. (3 Elliot 512)

6. Francis Corbin: Abuse of power. (3 Elliot 516)

Checks Upon General Powers of Congress

The following is a partial summary and paraphrase of statements made during the State ratification debates concerning the checks upon Congress for abuse of any of its powers. This material is derived from the broader compilation of impeachment discussion in the next section.

Massachusetts Convention:

1. Mr. Ames: Electing one-third of the Senate every two years. (2 Elliot 46-47)

2. Mr. Bowdoin: Impeachment of Members of Congress. (2 Elliot 85-86)

3. Mr. Stillman: Impeachment of Members of Congress. (2 Elliot 168-169)

4. Gen. Brooks: Impeachment of Senators. (2 Elliot 45)

Connecticut Convention:

1. Oliver Ellsworth (a delegate at the Constitutional Convention): Judicial review of legislative acts. (2 Elliot 196)

Pennsylvania Convention:

1. James Wilson (a leading delegate to the Constitutional Convention): Dividing the legislative power between two bodies; judicial review of legislative acts; regarding the Senate's power

64

try impeachments, the requirement that the
House first impeach; self-restraint. (2
Elliot 445-446, 476-477, 478, 489, 504-505)

2. Mr. M'Kean: Regarding impeachment trials,
    Senators acting under the sanction of an oath
    or affirmation. (2 Elliot 530, 534-535)

New York Convention:

1. Chancellor Livingston: Regarding the Senate's
    power to try impeachments, the requirement that
    the House first impeach. (2 Elliot 323)

South Carolina Convention:

1. Charles Pinckney (a delegate to the Constitu-
    tional Convention): Dividing the legislative
    power between two bodies. (4 Elliot 257)

2. Judge Pendleton: Senators need to be subject
    to a provision like impeachment. (4 Elliot
    263)

3. Edmund Rutledge: Senators impeachable. (4
    Elliot 276)

North Carolina Convention:

1. Mr. Maclaine: Regarding the Senate's power to
    try impeachments of the President, the presence
    of the Chief Justice, the two-thirds vote needed
    for conviction, and the requirement of voting

under oath; the people would check unconsti-

tutional acts. (4 Elliot 44-45, 47, 161-162)

2. Mr. Iredell: The House of Representatives

would serve to check the Senate's powers;

the people would check unconstitutional acts.

(4 Elliot 129, 132-134, 171-172)

Virginia Convention:

1. John Marshall: The power of judicial review

over legislative enactments. (3 Elliot 553)

2. Mason and Patrick Henry: Feared Senate would

not convict impeached Senators. (3 Elliot 402-

403, 512)

3. Convention as a whole: Recommended amendment

to provide for an independent body to try

impeached Senators. (3 Elliot 661)

3.   Compilation of Statements in State Ratification
      Debates Relevant to Controlling Power and Officers

Massachusetts: Mr. Ames, defending a two-year term

for House members, noted that:

> representatives are the grand inquisition of the Union.
> They are, by impeachment, to bring great offenders to
> justice. One year will not suffice to detect guilt
> and to pursue it to conviction; therefore they will
> escape, and the balance of the two branches will be
> destroyed, and the people oppressed with impunity.
> (2 Elliot 11)

Dr. Taylor, opposing biennial and favoring annual elections

of House members, stated that

> [I]t is possible that rulers may be appointed who may
> wish to root out the liberties of the people. Is it
> not . . . better, if such a case should occur, that at
> a short period they should politically die, than that
> they should be proceeded against by impeachment? (2
> Elliot 5)

General Brooks stated that if Senators' "conduct excites

suspicion, they are to be impeached. . ." (2 Elliot 45)

Mr. Ames stated that a very effectual check upon the

powers of the Senate was the provision requiring one-third

of its members to be elected every two years. (2 Elliot 46-47)

Mr. Bowdoin cited the impeachment provisions in Art. II,

§4 as a check against the abuse of power. (2 Elliot 85-86)

Mr. Stillman, defending the proposed Constitution, stated

that its impeachment provisions were a "check in favor of the

people" and that every officer of Congress could be impeached

for "malconduct." He argued that "[W]ith such a prospect,

who will dare t abuse the powers vested in im by the people."
(Elliot 168-169)

> Connecticut: Oliver Ellsworth stated that if Congress:
>
> should at any time overlap their limits, the judicial
> department is a constitutional check. If the United
> States go beyond their powers, if they make a law
> which the Constitution does not authorize, it is
> void; and the judicial power . . . will declare it
> to be void. (Elliot 196)

> Maryland: The Maryland Convention, in ratifying the

Constitution, resolved that an amendment be adopted stating

that "Congress shall exercise no power but what is expressly

delegated by this Constitution." (2 Elliot 550)

Luther Martin, opposing ratification, criticized the

impeachment provision giving the Senate authority to try

impeachments on the ground that the Senate would be partial

towards the President. The Senate would receive many Presi-

dential favors and would participate in some his actions.

Additionally, the Chief Justice would be partial to the

President having been appointed by him. (3 Farrand 219)

He also discounted the impeachment power as a check upon

the executive and referred to "misconduct" as a basis for

impeachment:

> If he [the President] is guilty of misconduct
> and impeached for it by the first branch of the
> Legislature he must be tried in the second, and
> if he keeps an interest in the large States, he
> will always escape punishment -- The impeachment
> can rarely come from the Second branch, who are
> his Council and will be under his influence. (3
> Farrand 158)

James McHenry, stated that the Senate was given the power to try impeachments because it would be a less partisan and inflamed jury than the House. (3 Farrand 147-148)

Pennsylvania: James Wilson stated that the political
theory behind the Constitution was that all powers not expressly given were withheld and thus a bill of rights would
be superfluous and even dangerous by suggesting the federal
Government possessed powers that did not exist.   (2 Elliot
435-436)   In discussing the restraints upon Congress, he
mentioned the division of legislative power into two bodies,
election of members by the people, and the interposition of
the judicial department.   Regarding that latter check, he
stated that it was the duty of judges to pronounce legislation
inconsistent with the Constitution void.   (2 Elliot 445-446)
However, in discussing checks upon the powers of the Senate which
he thought were too great, Wilson stated that the Senate could
do nothing without the concurrence of some other branch of
government.   Regarding the power to try impeachments, he noted
that the Senate could not try unless the House impeached.
Although not approving in toto these impeachment provisions,
Wilson thought that "no danger to the liberties of this country
can arise even from that part of the system."   (2 Elliot 476-477,
see also, 2 Elliot 504-504)

Wilson asserted that making bad treaties would justify
impeachment of Senators.   (2 Elliot 477)   Judges were not to
be impeached for declaring acts of Congress null and void.
However, the guard against impeachment of judges for performing

their duties, Wilson suggested, was self-restraint by the House and Senate: "What House of Representatives would dare to impeach, or Senate to convict, judges for the performance of their duty?" (2 Elliot 478)

In discussing checks upon the power of the President, Wilson stated that "far from being above the laws, he is amenable to them in his private character as a citizen, and in his public character by impeachment." (Emphasis in original) (2 Elliot 480)

In discussing the judicial power, Wilson stated that courts would have the power to declare laws null and void if contrary to the Constitution. (2 Elliot 489) In discussing the federal judicial powers, Wilson neither stated nor implied a power of judicial review in connection with impeachment trials. (2 Elliot 486-494) Wilson admitted that the Senate possessed "executive" and "judicial" powers that violated separation of powers principles but asserted that nevertheless there existed "real and effectual security" to check those powers.

In discussing the impeachment powers of the Senate, Wilson stated that he hoped impeachment trials would "seldom happen." (2 Elliot 513)

Mr. M'Kean, in responding to the criticism that the Senate's power to try impeachments blended the legislative and judicial departments, stated that on the trial, "the Senators are to be under the sanction of an oath or affirmation, besides the other ties upon them to do justice; and the basis [sic] is more likely to be against the officer accused than in his favor, for there are always more persons disobliged, than the contrary, when an office is given away, and the expectants of office are more numerous than the possessors." (2 Elliot 530, 534-535)

Mr. M'Kean also stated that the President "may be impeache before the Senate, and punished for his crimes." (2 Elliot 538)

New York: Mr. Chancellor Livingston, refuting the contention that the Senate possessed too much power, including the power to try impeachments, stated that the:

> power of impeaching was in the House of Representatives, and that was the important power. It could hardly be supposed that the representatives would exercise this power for purposes of tyranny; but if they should, it certainly could be of no disadvantage to enable the Senate to check them. (2 Elliot 323)

The New York Convention recommended to other States that the following be adopted as an amendment after the Constitution was ratified: "that the Congress should appoint, in such manner as they may think proper, a council to advise the President in the appointment of officers; that the said council should continue in office for four years; that they should keep a record of their proceedings, and sign the same, and always be responsible for their advice, and impeachable for malconduct in office. . ." (2 Elliot 408)

South Carolina: Mr. Charles Pinckney stated that the purpose of establishing two houses of Congress whose members were elected by different constituents was "to introduce the influence of different interests and principles" in the actions of Congress. (4 Elliot 257)

Judge Pendleton, criticizing the Senate's power to try impeachments, stated that in "England, particularly, ministers that advised illegal measures were liable to impeachment, for advising the King. Now, if justice called for punishment of treachery in the Senate, on account of giving bad advice, before what tribunal could they be arraigned? Not surely before their house, that was absurd to suppose. Nor could the President be impeached for making treaties, he acting only under advice of the Senate, without a power of negativing." (4 Elliot 263)

John Rutledge, defending the treaty-making provisions, stated that the President would not join with a few Senators to make a bad treaty impinging upon individual liberty, because a "full Senate were competent to impeach him." (4 Elliot 268)

Edward Rutledge stated that both the President and Senators were impeachable for abuse of trust. (4 Elliot 276)

General Charles Pinckney stated that the House of Representatives "are to impeach those who behave amiss, or betray their public trust. . ." (4 Elliot 281) He added that the President was not elected by the legislature because this power coupled with its impeaching power would make the President too dependent upon that Branch and unable to check legislative excesses. (4 Elliot 304)

North Carolina: Mr. Joseph Taylor objected to the Senate as a trier of impeachments because "the senators were liable to errors, especially in a case in which they themselves were concerned." (4 Elliot 32)

Mr. Iredell stated that "vesting the power of impeachment in the House of Representatives, is one of the greatest securities for a due execution of all public offices." He added that the impeaching power "will be not only the means of punishing misconduct, but will prevent misconduct." (Id.)

Mr. Taylor again objected to the impeachment provisions because "the impeachments are to be determined by the Senators, who are one of the branches of power which we dread under this Constitution." (4 Elliot 33)

Mr. Maclaine stated that an impeachment tribunal was to try "great offenses", and that impeachment was necessary to keep officers "within proper bounds." He added that Members of Congress, while not impeachable, were "amenable to the law for crimes and misdemeanors committed as individuals." (4 Elliot 34)

Mr. J. Taylor characterized impeachable acts as official acts of "oppression" against the people. (4 Elliot 36)

Mr. Maclaine stated that impeachments are only for high crimes and misdemeanors and would not reach petty offenses committed by tax collectors. (4 Elliot 37)

Mr. Iredell stated that officers may be tried by a court "for common law offenses, whether impeached or not." (Id.)

Mr. Maclaine stated that petty officers would not be impeached for every petty offense; that impeachments would not reach inferior officers because such a construction would depart from past British and American practice. The House of Representatives, the grand inquest of the Union at large, will bring "great offenders" to justice. Impeachment trials "will be a kind of state trial for high crimes and Misdemeanors." He observed that checks upon abuse of the Senate's power to try impeachments against the President were the presence of the Chief Justice, the two-thirds majority vote needed for conviction, and the requirement of voting under oath. The President was impeachable for his own "misdemeanors" or for any "maladministration" in his office. He added that notwithstanding the impeachment provisions, "there is not a single officer but may tried and indicted at common law. . ." (4 Elliot 44-45, 47)

Governor Johnston stated that "[i]f an officer commits crimes against the State, he may be indicted and punished. Impeachment only extends to high crimes and misdemeanors in a public office. It is a mode of trial pointed out for great misdemeanors against the public." (Emphasis in original) (4 Elliot 48)

Mr. Iredell, in explaining why no comparable King's Council was needed in the Constitution to prevent the abuse of executive power as in England, stated that if the President does a single act by which "the people are prejudiced", he is punishable himself. If he commits any "misdemeanor" in office, he is impeachable. If commits any "crime", he is punishable by the laws of his country. Because the President had no council, he would personally have the credit of good, or the censure of bad measures. (4 Elliot 109-110)

Iredell observed that impeachment was to be used to bring "great offenders" to "punishment for crime which it is not easy to describe, but which every one must be convinced is a high crime and misdemeanor against the government." The House was given the power to impeach "because the occasion for its exercise will arise from acts of great injury to the community, and the objects of it may be such as cannot be easily reached by an ordinary tribunal. The trial belongs to the Senate, lest an inferior tribunal should be too much awed by so powerful an accuser. . ." Iredell added that "the person convicted upon impeachment is further liable to a trial at common law, and may receive such common law punishment as

76

belongs to a description of such offenses, if it be punishable by that law." (4 Elliot 113-114)

Mr. Spaight stated that the President was impeachable if he "in any manner abused his trust." (4 Elliot 114)

Mr. Spencer objected to the Senate as the trier of impeachments because it violated the doctrine that each branch should be independent. He also objected to the absence of a President's Council. If one existed, each member "might be impeached, tried, and condemned for any misdemeanor in office." He again criticized the Senate as the trier of impeachments because often the President's challenged conduct would have received prior Senate concurrence. Thus, the Senate would never convict "for any misdemeanor in his office" unless for high treason, or unless they wish to fix the odium of any measure on him to exculpate themselves, which would never happen. (4 Elliot 116-118) He thought that the powers of the Senate including the power to try impeachments, were too great. (4 Elliot 118)

Mr. Davie, discussing the blending of powers under the Constitution, observed that the Senate is to "try impeachments. This is their only judicial cognizance. As to the ordinary objects of a judiciary - such as the decisions of controversies, the trial of criminals, etc. -- the judiciary is perfectly separate and distinct from the legislative and executive branches." (4 Elliot 121)

Mr. Spaight stated that the President may be impeached and punished for giving his consent to a treaty whereby the interest of the community is manifestly sacrificed. (4 Elliot 124)

Mr. Spencer contended that if the President was impeached for making a bad treaty, the Senate would not "pronounce sentence against him because they advised him to make it." (4 Elliot 124-125)

Mr. Iredell stated that the President could only be impeached for an abuse of trust; that impeachment lies only "for an error of the heart, and not of the head." He stated that the impeachment powers answered every purpose of people jealous of their liberty. If a man wilfully abuse his trust, he is to be held up as a public offender and punished. He stated that "I suppose the only instances in which the President would be liable to impeachment would be where he had received a bribe, or had acted from some corrupt motive or other." The President could be impeached for receiving a bribe from a foreign power and under the influence of that bribe, by artifice and misrepresentation, seduce the Senate's consent to a pernicious treaty. He asserted that the "President must certainly be punishable for giving false information to the Senate." Iredell doubted whether legislators were impeachable. He indicated that impeachment of legislators would be pernicious because legislative faction and suspicion would prevail; it would be a check upon the public business. If a Senator was impeachable, it could "only be for corruption, or some other wicked motive. . ." (4 Elliot 126-128)

Iredell compared the blending of the different branches of powers in the Senate (including the power to try impeachments) and its consequent danger with the powers of the House of Lords and concluded no fear was justified He mentioned that the House of Representatives would serve as a check upon the Senate's powers. (4 Elliot 129)

Mr. Spencer stated that the Senate would not be the proper tribunal to try impeachments of its own members, and that it might unjustly convict a President to throw the odium of a bad treaty upon him. He thought that the Senate's powers, were not sufficiently guarded. (4 Elliot 131-132)

Mr. Iredell again mentioned the House of Representatives as a check upon the power of the Senate and President. (4 Elliot 132-134)

Mr. Maclaine and Governor Johnston asserted that Congress could exercise only enumerated powers (4 Elliot 140, 142)

Mr. Davie, in discussing the powers of the federal judiciary, asserted that it had the authority to hold State laws unconstitutional. He stated that the judiciary had the power to enforce obedience to the Constitution and that the federal judicial power was properly coextensive with the federal legislative power. (4 Elliot 156-158)

Mr. Maclaine and Mr. Iredell indicated that the power to check unconstitutional acts was in the people. (4 Elliot 161-162, 171-172)

Iredell thought that the number of federal crimes would be very limited. (4 Elliot 219)

The North Carolina Convention proposed an amendment to the Constitution that would remove the Senate as the trier of impeachments against Senators. (4 Elliot 246)

Virginia: Mr. Nicholas, contending that the Constitutional impeachment provisions were an improvement over the similar British system as a check upon the executive stated:

> Another source of superiority is the power of impeachment. In England, very few ministers have dared to bring on themselves an accusation by the representatives of the people, by pursuing means contrary to their rights and liberties. Few ministers will ever run the risk of being impeached, when they know the king cannot protect them by a pardon. This power must have much greater force in America, where the President humself is personally amenable for his mal-administration; the power of impeachment must be a sufficient check on the President's power of pardoning before conviction. (3 Elliot 17)

Governor Randolph, mentioning checks upon the powers of the executive, stated that the President can be impeached if he "misbehaves." (3 Elliot 201)

Mr. Nicholas, mentioning impeachment as a check upon the executive, stated that the President would be disqualified from holding office and liable to further punishment if he committed such high crimes as are punishable at common law. (3 Elliot 240) He also asserted that Congress could exercise only enumerated powers. (3 Elliot 245-246)

Mr. Tyler contended that the Senate was too dangerous because of its treaty-making power and its power to try impeachments. (3 Elliot 366)

Governor Randolph asserted that the President may be impeached if he be "dishonest." (3 Elliot 368)

Patrick Henry, discussing British impeachment practice, stated that the British executed the highest officials for "mal-practices" and that impeachment follows quickly a violation of duty. (3 Elliot 397-398) He also contended that the federal courts would have the power to review legislative enactments.

Governor Randolph asserted that in England, no man could be impeached for an opinion. He stated that the making of a treaty was the most common occasion for impeachment. He also mentioned the difficulty in determining the "wilfulness" in giving a bad opinion which proof would be necessary for impeachment. (3 Elliot 401)

Mr. Mason objected that no proper court would be available to try Senators for indictable offenses. He stated that the Senate would not convict its own members upon impeachment for making a treaty after being bribed. (3 Elliot 402-403)

Governor Randolph stated that the President could be impeached for receiving foreign emoluments. (3 Elliot 486)

Mr. Mason feared that the Senate could always acquit the President in impeachment trials. (3 Elliot 494)

Mr. Madison, in discussing checks upon the President's power to pardon, stated that the President could be impeached for sheltering a suspicious man with whom he was connected. He added that, were the President to commit anything so atrocious as to summon only a few of the States' Senators to approve a treaty, he would be impeached for such a misdemeanor. (3 Elliot 498, 500) Madison, however, seemingly erroneously stated in discussing checks upon the President's power, that the House could suspend the President upon impeachment. (3 Elliot 496-498) (That proposal was specifically rejected by the Constitutional Convention, after Madison stated his objection that such power to suspend would make the executive too dependent upon the legislature).

Mr. Nicholas, citing Blackstone, stated that ministers concluding bad treaties for criminal motives could be impeached. (3 Elliot 506)

Patrick Henry opined that the Senate would never convict its own members upon impeachment for making bad treaties. (3 Elliot 512)

Madison stated that in England, ministers were impeachable for advising the King to abuse the royal perogative. He added that the President could be impeached for the same abuses. (3 Elliot 516)

Mr. Pendleton stated that the federal judicial power was coextensive with the federal legislative power. (3 Elliot 517)

John Marshall stated that federal courts would have the power of judicial review over legislative enactments. (3 Elliot 553)

Governor Randolph and Madison both asserted that the federal government could only exercise those powers enumerated in the Constitution. (3 Elliot 576, 620)

Mr. Henry implied that the minister who will sacrifice the interest of the nation is subject to impeachment. (3 Elliot 512)

Francis Corbin stated that an abuse of power by the President was impeachable conduct. (3 Elliot 516)

After ratifying the Constitution, Virginia recommended that an amendment be adopted that would substitute a different tribunal than the Senate for trying impeachments of Senators. (3 Elliot 661)

C. State Constitutions

State constitutional impeachment provisions shed little light on the impeachment questions addressed in this memorandum.

1. Background

The thirteen original States all had constitutions in effect during or shortly after 1787, providing for impeachment or comparable proceedings against certain officials.

Connecticut[57] provided that certain officials appointed by the Charter Company (composed of several members) be removed by "misdemeanor or default" by the Governor, Assistants and the Company in public courts to be assembled.

Delaware[58] provided for impeachment of the President when out of office and within 18 months thereafter, and all others offending against the State, either by maladministration, corruption, or other means by which the safety of the Common-wealth may be endangered. The house of assembly was to impeach with trial by the legislative council, the upper legislative

---

57/ 1 B. Poore, the Federal and State Constitutions, Colonial Charters, and Other Organic Laws of the United States (2d. ed. 1878), at 254 (hereinafter cited as Poore's). (1776 Constitution).

58/ 1 Poore's 274, 276-77. (1776 Constitution)

branch. Punishment upon conviction was either perpetual disqualification from holding office or provisional removal from
office. Additionally, all officers were to be removed on
conviction of misbehavior at common law, impeachment, or upon
the address of the general assembly. The President was elected
by the legislature, for a three-year term.

In Georgia [59/], the House of Delegates had the sole power
to impeach all persons who have been or may be in office.
The Senate had all power to try impeachments. The Governor
was elected by the Legislature for a two-year term.

In Maryland [60/], judges were to be removed for misbehavior
or conviction in a court of law, or by the Governor, upon the
address of the General Assembly.

In Massachusetts [61/], the Senate was to try impeachments
voted by the House against any officer for misconduct and
maladministration in office. The Governor was elected independently from the legislature for one year.

59/
 1 Poore's 384-385. (1789 Constitution)
60/
 1 Poore's 819.   (1776 Constitution)
61/
 1 Poore's 963-964.   (1780 Constitution)

New Hampshire[62] had virtually the same provisions for impeachment as Massachusetts, and a comparable method of electing the chief magistrate.

In New York[63], all officers could be impeached for mal and corrupt conduct and tried before the president of the senate, senators, the chancellor, and judges of the supreme court. Punishment upon conviction was limited to removal and disqualification as in the Federal Constitution. Counsel was specifically provided a party impeached. The Governor was elected by the people for a three-year term.

In North Carolina[64], the Governor, and other officers, offending against the State by violating any part of the Constitution, by maladministration, or by corruption could be prosecuted upon impeachment by the General Assembly or grand jury presentment. The Governor was chosen by the Legislature for one year.

In Pennsylvania[65], every officer was liable to be impeached by the general assembly when in office or after resignation for mal-administration. Impeachments were to be tried before the

---

[62] 2 Poore's 1286-1287. (1794 Constitution)

[63] 2 Poore's 1312-1313. (1776 Constitution)

[64] 2 Poore's 1335, 1337. (1777 Constitution)

[65] 2 Poore's 1412, 1413. (1776 Constitution)

president or vice-president and council (an elected executive body). The president was chosen by the assembly and council for one year.

In Rhode Island [66], officers were removable for any misdemeanor or default by the Governor, Assistants and the Company (composed of several governing members).

In South Carolina [67], officers were to be impeached by the House for mal and corrupt conduct and tried by Senators and judges. The party accused was specifically allowed counsel. The Governor was chosen from and by the Legislature for a two-year term.

In Virginia [68], the Governor, when out of office, and others, offending against the State were to be impeached by the House of Delegates for mal-administration, corruption, or other means by which the safety of the State may be endangered. The Governor was elected by the Legislature for one year. Judges of the General Court who were impeached were to be tried in the Court of Appeals.

---

[66] 2 Poore's 1545.   (1776 Constitution)

[67] 2 Poore's 1599.   (1663 Charter)

[68] 2 Poore's 1621, 1624-1625.   (1778 Constitution)

2. Grounds for Impeachment

Contemporaneous State Constitutional provisions offer
little aid in determining what was meant by "high crimes
and misdemeanors" in Art. II, §4 of the United States Constitution. At the Constitutional Convention the phrase "high
crimes and misdemeanors" was substituted, for "maladministration,"
a justification for impeachment in several State Constitutions
at that time. Maladministration was opposed as too "vague"
by Madison, who presumably knew of experience with that term
in Virginia which authorized impeachment for that behavior.
No State Constitution provided for impeachment for high crimes
and misdemeanors. That the Convention delegates presumably
knew of "maladministration" or the like as a basis for impeachment in State constitutions and rejected that concept
in favor of a more rigorous standard of misconduct for Federal
impeachments suggests that to constitute a "high crime or
misdemeanor" more than simple incompetency in office is
required. Nothing more can reasonably be inferred from contemporaneous State Constitutional impeachment provisions.

3. Judicial Review

No State Constitutional provisions expressly provided
for judicial review of impeachment proceedings. This fact
could permit an inference that no judicial review of Federal

impeachment proceedings was contemplated. It may be contended that the Convention delegates, knowing that judicial review of impeachments in States was not available would have expressly provided for judicial review if they intended to depart from accepted State procedures. However, research revealed no indication of whether judicial review of State impeachment proceedings was impliedly permitted under State law at the time of the drafting of the United States Constitution. Without such knowledge any inference to be drawn from State practice is hazardous. In addition, it may be observed that of all of our constitutional institutions, the institution of judicial review has had the most significant post-Convention development.

Department of Justice

LEGAL ASPECTS OF IMPEACHMENT: An Overview

Appendix III: Historical Statements on
Executive Privilege and Impeachment

This appendix is a working paper prepared by the staff of the Office of Legal Counsel. The views expressed should not be regarded as an official position of the Department of Justice.

Robert G. Dixon, Jr.
Assistant Attorney General
Office of Legal Counsel

APPENDIX III

Summary of Discussion

1. Precedents relating to the subject of executive
privilege in presidential impeachment are meager, confused
and inconclusive. Views expressed by Attorneys General are
not in agreement, and may in part at least be said to be
dicta. In the only impeachment of a President in the
Nation's history, Andrew Johnson did not appear to give
testimony and he did not assert the claim of executive
privilege. We are not aware of any impeachment involving a
federal official (including William W. Belknap, Secretary
of War, 1876) where executive privilege was invoked. Because almost all of the other cases involved judges, however,
there may have been no occasion to assert it. In the Justice
Douglas impeachment investigation of 1970, President Nixon
stated that the executive branch was "clearly obligated"
to supply relevant information to the legislative branch
"to the extent compatible with the public interest." The

Department of Justice accordingly made available to the Committee "raw" FBI files.

Some presidential statements, declining to make available information requested by congressional committees in nonimpeachment contexts, have included the observation that only in an impeachment proceeding can the President be held to an accounting of his conduct. Other presidential statements imply this conclusion but are open to conflicting interpretations. It is unclear from many of these statements whether the President's power to invoke executive privilege in an impeachment proceeding is deemed nonexistent or merely subject to extraordinary restraint.

Conceivably in impeachment by the House or in the trial by the Senate, the President may feel that it is his constitutional duty not to disclose certain information which may endanger national security or the conduct of foreign affairs. It is unclear how the propriety of the President's refusal to make such information available may be tested. Perhaps in camera techniques could be employed by the Chief Justice, who is the presiding officer at a presidential impeachment trial, as was done by Judge Sirica in respect to the recent Watergate grand jury subpoenas. A Chief Justice ruling that the President may decline to disclose might then be overridden

-2-

by the Senate, following established custom that the Senate has the last word on admissibility of evidence. If the President persisted in his refusal to comply, a constitutional confrontation of the highest magnitude would ensue.

Executive Privilege in Impeachment

The material which follows deals with the question whether the doctrine of executive privilege may be relied on by the President in a House impeachment or subsequent Senate trial. It is drawn from various sources, as follows:

1. Statements by Attorneys General made in the course of litigation, formal opinions, and testimony before congressional committees.

2. Statements by the attorneys for the President in the recent Watergate litigation.

3. Statements made by Presidents in resisting congressional committee demands for information or on other occasions.

It is important to note at the outset what executive privilege is. It derives from the separation of powers and is a privilege asserted by the Executive to avert the harms to the public which could ensue from disclosure, or premature disclosure, of certain types of governmental information. Sparingly used, the major categories have been national security information particularly in the areas of military affairs and foreign policy, law enforcement investigatory data, and

internal opinions and advice (as distinct from decisions) received from presidential advisers. $\underline{*/}$

---

*/ Testimony of Attorney General Richard G. Kleindienst on
"Executive Privilege," etc., Hearings before the Subcommittee
on Intergovernmental Relations of the Committee on Government
Operations, and the Subcommittees on Separation of Powers and
Administrative Practice and Procedure of the Committee on the
Judiciary, U.S. Senate, 93d Cong., 1st Sess., on S. 1142, etc.
(1973), 20-23, (referred to hereafter as the "1973 Hearings").

I. Statements of Attorneys General

A. Attorney General Stanbery (1866)

Mississippi v. Johnson, President [1]

A motion was made by the State of Mississippi to file a suit in the Supreme Court to enjoin Andrew Johnson as citizen and as President of the United States, and also his subordinates, from carrying into effect the Reconstruction Acts upon the ground that they were unconstitutional. The Supreme Court denied the motion to file the bill for the reason that it lacked jurisdiction to enjoin the President in the performance of his official duties. In opposing the suit, Attorney General Stanbery argued that the President is above the process of any court or the jurisdiction of any judicial tribunal to bring him to account as President. However, Stanbery said: [2]

> There is only one court or quasi court that he can be called upon to answer to for any derelic-tion of duty, for doing anything that is contrary to law or failing to do anything which is accord-ing to law, and that is not this tribunal but one that sits in another chamber of this capitol. /Impeachment7. There he can be called and tried and punished, but not here while he is President
> . . . .

1/ 4 Wall, 475 (1866).

2/ Id., 484-485.

-6-

In elaborating on this point, Stanbery argued further as follows: 3/

> The view I maintain has been expressed in this
> court, so far as the President is concerned. In
> Kendall v. United States. (12 Pet. 524, 609
> (1833):
>
> > The executive power is vested in the
> > President. As far as his power is
> > derived from the Constitution he is
> > beyond the reach of any other depart-
> > ment, except in the mode prescribed by
> > the Constitution--through the impeach-
> > ing power.
>
> There it is. As President, he is beyond the con-
> trol of any other department, except through the
> impeaching power. For what is he reached by the
> impeaching power? The highest crimes and mis-
> demeanors. Therefore, according to this, for the
> highest crimes and misdemeanors, he is, as Presi-
> dent, above the power of any court or any other
> department of the government. Only in that other
> chamber can you arraign him for anything done or
> omitted to be done while he is President. (Under-
> scoring added.)

In this suit there was no occasion by Attorney General Stanbery

to reach the point whether, and to what extent, the President

could rely on the defense of executive privilege in refusing

to make available information in an impeachment proceeding

3/ Id., at 491. The Court limited its inquiry to the question
presented by the objection that the bill sought to enjoin the
President in the performance of his duties as President. It
disclaimed expressing any opinion on the broader issues raised
in argument whether the President may be required "by the process
of this Court, to perform a purely ministerial act under a positive law, or may be held amenable, in any case, otherwise than
by impeachment for crime." 4 Wall at 498.

against him. However, in the subsequent impeachment of President Johnson, where Stanbery was one of three attorneys who represented Johnson,[4/] no attempt was made to rely on the doctrine of executive privilege or any related defense in resisting the impeachment. Johnson did <u>not</u> appear personally to testify before the Senate.

B. <u>Attorney General Jackson (1941)</u>

In 1941, the Department of Justice was requested by the Chairman, House Committee on Naval Affairs, to furnish all Federal Bureau of Investigation reports since June 1939, together with all future reports, memoranda, and correspondence of the FBI, or the Department of Justice, in connection with investigations made by the Department arising out of strikes, subversive activities in connection with labor disputes or disturbances in industrial establishments which had naval contracts. In declining to make these materials available, Attorney General Jackson stated that it was the Department's position, "with the approval of and at the direction of the

---

4/ The Senate trial of the impeachment began on March 13, 1868. Stanbery, who was strongly loyal to Johnson, resigned as Attorney General on March 12, 1868, just before the trial began "to prevent public duties from interfering with his handling of the case and also to avoid criticism." Cummings and McFarland Federal Justice (1937), 215. Stanbery and all the other members of the President's defense counsel "donated their services." Lomask, <u>Andrew Johnson: President on Trial</u> (1960), 280.

-8-

President," that all investigative reports are confidential documents of the executive department of the Government to aid in the duty imposed on the President by the Constitution "to take care that the laws be faithfully executed," and that congressional or public access to them would not be in the public interest. 5/

However, Attorney General Jackson stated that where the public interest has seemed to justify it, information as to particular matters has been supplied to congressional committees by him and by former Attorneys General. By way of illustration, the Attorney General said: 6/

> I have taken the position that committees called upon to pass on the confirmation of persons recommended for appointment by the Attorney General would be afforded confidential access to any information that we have--because no candidate's name is submitted without his knowledge and the Department does not intend to submit the name of any person whose entire history will not stand light. By way of further illustration, I may mention that pertinent information would be supplied in impeachment proceedings, usually instituted at the suggestion of the Department and for the good of the administration of justice. (Underscoring added.)

C. Attorney General Rogers (1958)

In his general discussion of the scope of executive privilege, former Attorney General Rogers stated that nondisclosure can "never be justified as a means of covering mistakes, avoiding

5/ 40 Ops. A.G. 45, 46 (1941).

6/ Id., at 51.

embarrassment, or for political, personal or pecuniary reasons."[7]
It is not clear whether Mr. Rogers intended to include an impeachment proceeding as among those situations in which executive privilege could not be claimed.

D. Attorney General Kleindienst (1973)

In hearings before congressional committees on executive privilege, former Attorney General Kleindienst expressed the view that the President could assert executive privilege to prevent his confidential advisers from testifying in an impeachment proceeding against him. This rationale appears to have been based on Mr. Kleindienst's strong concept of separation of powers, and the ultimate power of Congress to work its will in impeachment without the restraint of judicial review.[8] In the course of his testimony, Mr. Kleindienst, in answer to questions, said that Congress has a remedy in the form of an impeachment if the President were subpoenaed to appear before the Congress to testify, whether it was "a

_____

7/ Rogers, Constitutional Law: The Papers of the Executive Branch, 44 A.B.A.J. 941 (1958).

8/ Executive privilege, etc.; Hearings before the Subcommittee on Intergovernmental Relations of the Committee on Government Operations and the Subcommittees on Separation of Powers and Administrative Practice and Procedure of the Committee on the Judiciary, U.S. Senate, 93d Cong., 1st Sess. on S. 1142, etc. (1973), 45 (referred to hereafter as the "1973 Hearings").

criminal matter or any other matter," and if he refused to
do so. $\underline{9/}$ The following colloquy then took place between him
and Senator Roth. $\underline{10/}$

Senator Roth . . . .

You stated that it was your belief that any
evidence of wrongdoing should be reported to a
grand jury. This raises a question in my mind in
two areas if one agrees with that fundamental
proposition. One would be what would happen in
the case of impeachment proceedings. When I was
on the House side there was an effort to bring
about impeachment proceedings for a member of the
Supreme Court. Would the House have the right in
such a case to procure evidence or information with
respect to charges affecting a man's right to continue to hold office?

Mr. Kleindienst. In an impeachment proceeding?

Senator Roth. Yes.

Mr. Kleindienst. Where they are impeaching the
President of the United States--

Senator Roth. Not necessarily the President, an
officeholder; a judge for example.

Mr. Kleindienst. If you are conducting an impeachment proceeding based upon high crimes and misdemeanors and you want to subpoena someone from the
President's staff to give you information, I believe
that, based upon the doctrine of separation of powers,
the President would have the power to invoke executive
privilege with respect to that information.

9/ Id., 42.

10/ Id., 39.

-11-

Senator Roth. So that the executive privilege would still prevail even in those circumstances?

Mr. Kleindienst. Yes, in my opinion.

At a later point, there was the following colloquy between Senator Ervin and Mr. Kleindienst. [11]/

Senator Ervin. If you will pardon the interjection, I think under your interpretation there would be no danger of the President's being impeached because he could forbid any witnesses to testify before the Senate or court.

Mr. Kleindienst. I think you put a nice question, Senator Ervin, but you carried my hypothetical argument out to its logical extreme. If the only evidence necessary to impeach the President was contained in the bosom of his confidential adviser, I think his impeachment proceeding might not be predicated upon evidence. You do not need facts to impeach the President, because the Congress, if it has the votes, is the sole judge. The House passes a resolution, the Senate tries it, he is impeached, and there is no court of appeal. That is the end, with or without facts. (Underscoring added.)

Subsequently, Senator Muskie invited Mr. Kleindienst's attention to a statement made by President Polk in 1846 on the subject as follows: [12]/

If the House of Representatives is the grand inquest of the Nation and should at any time have reason to believe that there has been malversation in office and should think proper to institute an investigation into the matter, all the archives, public or private, would be subject to the inspection

---

11/ Id., 45.

12/ Id., 47.

and control of a committee of their body and
every facility in the power of the Executive
afforded them to prosecute the investigation.

Mr. Kleindienst stated that he disagreed with the views expressed by President Polk.[13/]

In a further exchange with Senator Ervin, Mr. Kleindienst
stated that "if you ever found a President who abused his
office, you have your remedy . . . and if the new President
abuses it, you can get another one."[14/] Finally, the following ensued:[15/]

> Senator Ervin. If the President forbids
> them to testify before the Senate, then the
> Senate would have no evidence with which to
> make adjudication.
>
> Mr. Kleindienst. You do not need evidence
> to impeach a President. You get the resolution
> passed by the House and trial by the Senate and
> if the Senate votes on that trial, and if the
> Senate agrees, he is impeached. That is the end
> of it.

In short, it was Mr. Kleindienst's view that the impera-
tives of executive privilege could not be overridden by impeachment, but also that invocation of privilege could not
immunize the President from impeachment and removal by a determined Congress.

13/ Id.

14/ Id., 54.

15/ Id., 51-52.

E.   Attorney General Richardson (1973)

In Mr. Richardson's testimony in the 1973 Hearings, after
he had replaced Mr. Kleindienst as Attorney General, he was
asked whether his opinion was the same as Attorney General
Kleindienst as to the scope of the executive privilege, viz:
"that the cloak of executive privilege could in effect be
thrown over anyone who was working within the executive
department at the whim of the President himself." Mr.
Richardson stated that he "wouldn't express it the same way,"
but in the event of "arbitrary action on the part of the
President . . . there would be no remedy presumably other
than impeachment or possibly some extraordinary writ issued
by a court."[16] In these hearings Mr. Richardson's testimony
did not touch on the point as to whether, if there were an
impeachment, the President could stand on executive privilege
in defending his innocence.

On November 6, 1973, Mr. Richardson testified before the
Senate Committee on the Judiciary, in hearings on a proposal
providing for appointment of a new special prosecutor. In
the course of his testimony, Mr. Richardson stated that "in
light of the sequence which resulted in the firing of Mr. Cox
over the issue of whether or not be would be allowed to seek
judicial process, and which was followed then by a complete

16/   1973 Hearings, supra, Vol. 2 (1973), 230.

-14-

reversal with respect to the availability of the tapes . . .,
we have reached the point where any further conversation about
/_executive_/privilege ought to be eliminated. . .." [17] Mr.
Richardson also stated that if the President refused to make a
commitment of yielding the tapes and presidential material,
"it would have to be taken into account as a part of the entire
situation the Nation now confronts." However, Mr. Richardson
made it clear that there was no "legal or constitutional way"
·by which such a commitment could be forced. [18]

Here again, it is not clear whether Mr. Richardson was
suggesting that the President should as a matter of sound
policy no longer stand on executive privilege in denying requests for information made by a court or the Special Prosecutor, or that if he continued to invoke privilege, impeachment
proceedings might follow. It is also unclear whether Mr.
Richardson believed the executive privilege would be unavailable to the President in the impeachment proceedings itself.

17/ Special Prosecutor, Hearings before the Committee on the
Judiciary, United States Senate, 93d Cong., 1st Sess. (1973),
Vol. I, 251-252.

18/ Id. To the extent that reliance on the executive privilege
rests on the doctrine of separation of powers, Berger is of the
view that when the Constitution gave Congress the impeachment
power, it constituted "a deliberate breach in the doctrine of
separation of powers, so that no argument drawn from that doctrine (such as executive privilege) may apply to the preliminary
inquiry by the House or the subsequent trial by the Senate."
Berger, Impeachment: Instrument of Regeneration, Harper's Maga-
zine, 14 (Jan. 1974).

II. Statements by Attorneys for the President
     in Recent Watergate Litigation

A. Brief of Attorneys for the President in Opposition
    to Grand Jury Subpoena to the President to Produce
    Certain Documents. Misc. No. 47-73 (D.C.D.C.) 19/

On July 23, 1973, at the direction of the Special Prosecutor, Watergate Special Prosecution Force, the clerk of the
district court issued a subpoena _duces tecum_ to the President directing him to produce certain documents before a
pending grand jury proceeding. Opposing an attempt by the
Special Prosecutor to enforce the subpoena, attorneys for
the President argued that the President has the privilege to
withhold information if he concludes (as he did) that the
disclosure would not be in the public interest. The President's attorneys quoted from Kendall v. United States ex rel.
Stokes, 12 Pet. (37 U.S.) 524, 610 (1838), where the Court
said that to the extent the President's powers are derived
from the Constitution, "he is beyond the reach of any other
department, except in the mode prescribed by the Constitution
through the impeaching power." (Underscoring added.)[20] Overruling the President's objections, the district court ordered
the President or any subordinate official to produce certain

_____

19/ 9 Weekly Compilation of Presidential Documents, 961 (1973).
20/ Id., 970.

-16-

subpoenaed items so that the court could determine by an in camera inspection whether the items were subject to executive privilege.[21/]

B. Brief of the Attorneys for the President in Richard M. Nixon, President v. Honorable John J. Sirica, U.S. District Judge and Archibald Cox, Special Prosecutor, etc. (D.C. Cir., No. 73-1962).

The President appealed to the Court of Appeals for the District of Columbia from Judge Sirica's order enforcing the subpoena against the President for the production of information and for in camera inspection, and overruling the President's claim of executive privilege. His attorneys criticized the district court's suggestion that an otherwise valid claim of privilege by the President could be overridden if the evidence sought would show that the President himself had been guilty of a crime. They argued that even if there were such evidence, it could not be relevant to the grand jury or district court proceedings because of the inability to indict a President "prior to impeachment."[22/] A recurring issue in the Convention debates, they said, was whether the President should be answerable to the courts or to the Senate. On the basis of these debates, the President's attorneys concluded that the President is answerable, not to the courts, but "to the Senate,

[21/]With some modifications the district court's order enforcing the grand jury subpoena duces tecum served on the President, was upheld on appeal to the Court of Appeals for the District of Columbia, Nixon v. Sirica, 487 F.2d 700 (D.C. Cir., 1973).

[22/] 9 Weekly Compilation of Presidential Documents, 1101, 1106 (1973).

sitting as a Court of Impeachment," and that "impeachment is the device that ensures that he is not above justice."[23] Once again the President's attorneys relied on Kendall v. United States ex rel. Stokes, 12 Pet. 524, 610, where the Court said that the President is "beyond the reach of any other department, except in the mode prescribed by the Constitution through its impeaching power."

It was conceded that executive privilege has limits. For example, the President's brief stated: "Executive privilege cannot be claimed to shield executive officers from prosecution for crime. Gravel v. United States, 408 U.S. 606, 627 (1972)."[24] The brief went on to add: "It is precisely with that consideration in mind, and with a strong desire that the truth about Watergate be brought out, that the President has not asserted executive privilege with regard to testimony about possible criminal conduct or discussions of possible criminal conduct." But the brief argued that testimony can be confined to the relevant portions of the conversations and be limited to matters that do not endanger national security.[25]

23/ Id.

24/ Id., 1116.

25/ Id.

The Court of Appeals rejected this argument on the
ground that the applicability of the privilege in any
given case is ultimately for the court and not the President
to decide.[26/] It concluded that when a claim of executive
privilege is challenged, it is for the court to assure
that the official who asserts the privilege has not "exceeded
his charter or flouted the legislative will." [27/] The Court
of Appeals stated that "although the views of the Chief
Executive on whether his executive privilege should obtain
are properly given the greatest weight and deference, they
cannot be conclusive."[28/]

Although also stating that the "Impeachment Clause does
not imply immunity from routine court process,"[29/] the Court
of Appeals did not reach or decide the question whether
executive privilege could prevail in an impeachment
proceeding.

26/   Nixon v. Sirica, supra, 487 F. 2d at 713.

27/   Id., at 714, quoting with approval from Nuclear
Responsibility, Inc. v. Seaborg, 463 F. 2d 788, 793
(D.C. Cir., 1971).

28/   Id., at 716.

29/   Id., at 711.

C. Brief of Attorneys for the President in Opposition to Motion of Senate Select Committee on Presidential Activities for an Order to Enforce Subpoena _Duces Tecum_ on the President.

Thereafter, the Senate Select Committee sought an order in the nature of a declaratory judgment that its subpoenas on the President must be honored, despite a claim of executive privilege. Attorneys for the President argued, _inter alia_, that the Committee had exceeded its legislative authority because its inquiry was not germane to the Committee's legislative purpose.[30/] They also argued that apart from impeachment, there was no authority, historical or legal, for the proposition that the President can be compelled to furnish information to the Congress for the purpose of eliciting evidence of the President's alleged criminal conduct. Claiming that the President is answerable solely in an impeachment proceeding, his attorneys summed up their conclusion as follows:[31/]

> One noteworthy characteristic of the plaintiff's argument is its candor. Few words are minced in delineating the central purpose of this proceeding: to discover evidence from the President's records, indeed from his own private conversations, that might establish Presidential complicity in the commission of serious crimes. Objections to legislative inquiry into the innocence or guilt of

---

30/ 9 _Weekly Compilation of Presidential Documents_, 1174 (1970).

31/ _Id._, 1105.

individuals are formidable in any case. <u>There is,</u>
<u>we submit, a categorical bar to compulsory process</u>
<u>designed to elicit evidence of criminal conduct on</u>
<u>the part of the President of the United States, for</u>
<u>he is answerable in only one constitutional pro-</u>
<u>ceeding. That proceeding requires the deliberate</u>
<u>action of the whole Congress under the Impeachment</u>
<u>Clause, not the filing of a discretionary suit by</u>
<u>a Select Committee of the Senate under a general</u>
<u>enabling resolution.</u> (Underscoring added.)

In the proceedings after remand,[32/] Judge Gesell brushed
aside a plea of nonjusticiability, and rejected the President's
assertion to a "blanket, unreviewable" claim of executive privilege. He nevertheless dismissed the Senate Watergate Committee's
suit to obtain five of the President's tapes in order "to safeguard pending criminal prosecutions from the possibly prejudicial
effect of pretrial publicity." The court stated, however (by way
of dictum), that congressional demands "for tapes in furtherance
of the more juridical constitutional process of impeachment would
present wholly, different considerations."

32/ On October 17, 1973, Judge Sirica dismissed this action
upon the ground that there was no statute conferring jurisdiction on the court to consider it. As a result of this
decision, Congress passed S. 2641 to provide the necessary
jurisdiction in the district court. 119 Cong. Rec. H 10484,
December 3, 1973 (Daily Ed.). The measure became law without the President's signature on December 18, 1973 (P.L. 93-
190). 9 Weekly Compilation of Presidential Documents, 1470
(1973). On the appeal from Judge Sirica's order of dismissal
in this action, the Court of Appeals remanded the cause to
the District Court for further proceedings in light of P.L.
93-190. Thereafter, the plaintiffs amended their complaint
to include the jurisdictional statement under P.L. 93-190.
Richard M. Nixon, individually and as President of the United
States, defendant in the action, filed a response to the
plaintiffs' memorandum on remand. 10 Weekly Compilation of
Presidential Documents, 45-61 (1974). In this response, the
President's attorneys relied on the defense of executive
privilege, but there is no discussion on the impeachment question. After remand, the matter was assigned to Judge Gesell,
whose memorandum and order, discussed above, was filed on
February 8, 1974. Senate Select Committee on Presidential
Campaign Activities v. Nixon, Civ. No. 1593-73 (D.C.C.), not
yet reported. He assumed, without significant discuss n, that a
congressional subpoena on the President was on the s. ne plane as
a judicial subpoena, and referred to Nixon v. Sirica, 487 F.2d
700 (D.C. Cir. 1973) which had enforced a judicial subpoena.

-21-

III. Presidential Precedents

A. Andrew Jackson

On February 10, 1835, President Andrew Jackson sent a Special Message to the Senate in reply to its Resolution requesting him to communicate copies of the charges, if any, made to him against the official conduct of Gideon Fitz, late surveyor general, which caused his removal from office. Jackson already had named Fitz's successor. Jackson stated that the President's power of removal from office is exclusive, and under the sanctions of his official oath "and of his liability to impeachment," he is bound to exercise this authority in the public interest. If from corrupt motives he abuses this power, he is also exposed to the same sanction. But Jackson stated "On no principle" can he be required to account for the manner in which he discharges this portion of his public duties, "save only in the mode and under the forms prescribed by the Constitution" (viz., impeachment).[33] (Underscoring added.) Jackson continued:[34]

> Besides, a compliance with the present resolution would in all probability subject the conduct and motives of the President in the case of Mr. Fitz to the review of the Senate when not sitting as judges on an impeachment, and even if this consequence should not occur in the present case the compliance of the Executive might hereafter be quoted as a

[33] 3 Messages and Papers of the Presidents, 1789-1897, 133.
[34] Id., 133-134.

-22-

precedent for similar and repeated applications.
Such a result, if acquiesced in, would ultimately
subject the independent constitutional action of
the Executive in a matter of great national con-
cernment to the domination and control of the
Senate; if not acquiesced in, it would lead to
collisions between coordinate branches of the
Government, well calculated to expose the parties
to indignity and reproach and to inflict on the
public interest serious and lasting mischief.

B.   James K. Polk

In 1846, during Polk's administration, the House of

Representatives requested an account of all payments made on

presidential certificates since 1841, particularly in connec-

tion with the Northeastern Boundary dispute. Polk noted the

strong public feeling which exists against secrecy of any

kind in the administration of the Government and especially

in reference to public expenditures, but it was his opinion

that foreign negotiations are wisely and properly confined

to the Executive during their pendency. Polk admitted, how-

ever, that under the power of impeachment the House had

power to "penetrate into most secret recesses of the Execu-

tive Departments."[35/] (Underscoring added.) In this connec-

tion, Polk said:[36/]

It may be alleged that the power of impeachment belongs to the House of Representatives, and that, with

_____

35/ 4 Richardson, Messages and Papers of the Presidents, 1799-
1897, 434.
36/ Id., 434-435.

-23-

a view to the exercise of this power, that House has the right to investigate the conduct of all public officers under the Government. This is cheerfully admitted. In such a case the safety of the Republic would be the supreme law, and the power of the House in the pursuit of this object would penetrate into the most secret recesses of the Executive Departments. It could command the attendance of any and every agent of the Government, and compel them to produce all papers, public or private, official or unofficial, and to testify on oath to all facts within their knowledge. But even in a case of that kind they would adopt all wise precautions to prevent the exposure of all such matters the publication of which might injuriously affect the public interest, except so far as this might be necessary to accomplish the great ends of public justice. If the House of Representatives, as the grand inquest of the Nation, should at any time have reason to believe that there has been malversation in office by an improper use or application of the public money by a public officer, and should think proper to institute an inquiry into the matter, all the archives and papers of the Executive Departments, public or private, would be subject to the inspection and control of a committee of their body and every facility in the power of the Executive be afforded to enable them to prosecute the investigation.37/ (Underscoring added.)

C.   James Buchanan

In 1860, the House of Representatives authorized a committee to investigate certain acts of President Buchanan alleged to constitute unlawful attempts to influence the Congress. The House called him to account for alleged attempts to defeat and

_____

37/   This statement by Polk has been interpreted by former presidential aid Arthur M. Schlesinger, Jr., as meaning that if the House of Representatives were conducting an inquiry with a view to impeachment, it could inspect the President's papers and require his personal testimony under oath. Schlesinger, "The Presidency and the Law," The Wall Street Journal, July 19, 1973; The Imperial Presidency (1973), 416. We question whether Polk's statement may be interpreted as to "require" the President's testimony under oath.

obstruct the proper execution of the laws. On March 28, 1860,
Buchanan filed a "Protest," rebuking the House for its actions
and arguing that impeachment was the only constitutional
device for such an inquiry. Buchanan said that "except in
this single case /Impeachment7, the Constitution has invested
the House of Representatives with no power, no jurisdiction,
no supremacy whatever over the President."[38]

Buchanan cited with approval the procedure which had
been invoked in the impeachment of Judge Peck in 1831, which
he ventured would "stand the test of time." Id. In that
case the accuser presented a petition to the House, setting
forth the charges in detail. The petition was referred to
the Judiciary Committee, which by composition and experience,
was qualified for the task of considering the charges. The
Committee heard witnesses who were subject to cross-examination,
and everything was conducted in such a manner as to afford
him (Judge Peck) no reasonable cause of complaint. In a
subsequent Message of June 22, 1860, to the House, Buchanan
again complained of the proceedings before the designated
special Committee rather than the Judiciary Committee for

38/ 5 Richardson, Messages and Papers of the Presidents,
1789-1897, 615.

impeachment purposes.^{39/} He pointed out that members of

the Senate "and members of my own Cabinet," and "both my

constitutional advisers" were called upon to testify for the

purpose of discovering anything to his discredit. Buchanan

deplored this "dragnet" going on "at the other end of the

avenue," the secrecy and odiousness of which was not even

exceeded by the Star-Chamber. Buchanan then pointed out

the difference in the function of the House acting in its

legislative role and in its impeachment role as follows:^{40/}

> Why should the House of Representatives desire to
> encroach on the other departments of the Government?
> Their rightful powers are ample for every legitimate
> purpose. They are the impeaching body. In their
> legislative capacity it is their most wise and
> wholesome prerogative to institute rigid examina-
> tions into the manner in which all departments of
> the Government are conducted, with a view to reform
> abuses, to promote economy, and to improve every
> branch of administration. Should they find reason
> to believe in the course of their examinations
> that any grave offense had been committed by the
> President or any officer of the Government rendering
> it proper, in their judgment, to resort to impeach-
> ment, their course would be plain. They would then
> transfer the question from their legislative to
> their accusatory jurisdiction, and take care that
> in all the preliminary judicial proceedings pre-
> paratory to the vote of articles of impeachment
> the accused should enjoy the benefit of cross-
> examining the witnesses and all the other safeguards
> with which the Constitution surrounds every American
> citizen. (Underscoring added.)

39/ Id., at 621.

40/ Id., 625.

D. Ulysses S. Grant

In 1876, after Grant had spent the preceding summer out
of Washington, the House of Representatives sought to embar-
rass him by inquiring whether any executive acts had been
performed away from the seat of government established by
law. Grant declined to provide this information, saying: [41/]

> I fail . . . to find in the Constitution of the
> United States the authority given to the House of
> Representatives (one branch of the Congress, in
> which is vested the legislative power of the Gov-
> ernment) to require of the Executive, an independent
> branch of the Government, coordinate with the Senate
> and House of Representatives, an account of his
> discharge of his appropriate and purely executive
> offices, acts and duties, either as to when, where,
> or how performed.
>
> What the House of Representatives may require
> as a right in its demand upon the Executive for
> information is limited to what is necessary for
> the proper discharge of its powers of legislation
> or of impeachment. (Underscoring added.)

E. Grover Cleveland

When Cleveland came into office, he suspended from office
certain existing officeholders who, it was claimed, had previously abused their authority for partisan purposes. The Senate
directed Department heads, particularly the Attorney General,
to transmit to it all documents relating to the conduct of

41/ 7 Richardson, Messages and Papers of the Presidents, 361,
362.

certain of these suspended officials. In answering this attempt to direct the action of his Cabinet officers, Cleveland sent a Special Message to the Senate on March 1, 1886, in which he stated that the power to remove or suspend such officials was vested in the President alone. He denied the right of the Senate to sit in judgment upon the exercise of his exclusive discretion in administering executive functions for which he was responsible solely to the people under the Constitution.

Cleveland stated that "I am not responsible to the Senate, and I am unwilling to submit my actions and official conduct to them for judgment."[42/] In declining to make the documents available, which are "not infrequently confidential," Cleveland stated that the Senate had no right to them "save through the judicial process of trial on impeachment to review or reverse the acts of the Executive in the suspension . . . of Federal officials."[43/] (Underscoring added.)

F. Theodore Roosevelt

In 1909, the Senate adopted a resolution directing the Attorney General to inform the Senate whether legal proceedings had been instituted by him against the United States Steel

---

42/ 8 Richardson, Messages and Papers of the Presidents, 375 382 (1886).

43/ Id., 379.

Corporation on account of its absorption of the Tennessee
Valley Coal and Iron Co. If no proceedings had been instituted, the Attorney General was to state the reasons for
his nonaction and if an opinion had been rendered by the
Attorney General respecting this transaction, he was to make
available a copy thereof. President Roosevelt stated that he
had been advised orally by the Attorney General that there
were insufficient grounds for legal proceedings against the
Steel Corporation. He also stated that he had given the Senate
all the information which appeared to him to be material
relevant to the subject of the resolution. He advised the
Senate that he had instructed the Attorney General not to re-
spond to the instructions of the Senate Resolution calling for
a statement of his reasons for nonaction.

Unable to obtain the documents from the Attorney General,
the Senate summoned Herbert Knox Smith, head of the Bureau of
Corporations, to appear before its Committee on the Judiciary.
When Smith appeared, the Committee informed him that if he
did not transmit the papers and documents requested, the
Senate would order his imprisonment. The President thereupon
ordered Mr. Smith to turn over to him all the papers in the
case. President Roosevelt then stated:[44/]

44/ Wolkinson, <u>Demands of Congressional Committees for Executive
Papers</u>, 10 Fed. B.J. 103, 128 (1948). The efforts to get the
papers took place in January 1909. Since Roosevelt's term expired
March 3, 1909, impeachment was highly remote. But a heated debate
in the Senate followed.

I have those papers in my possession, and last
night I informed Senator Clark of the Judiciary
Committee what I had done. I told him also that
the Senate should not have those papers and that
Herbert Knox Smith had turned them over to me.
The only way the Senate or the committee can get
those papers now is through my impeachment, and
I so informed Senator Clark last night. (Underscoring added.)

G. Richard M. Nixon

In 1970, a Special Subcommittee of the Committee on the

Judiciary, appointed under a resolution calling for the im-

peachment of Justice Douglas, asked the President, to the ex-

tent compatible with the public interest, to give it all

relevant reports, documents, and other data bearing on the

charges that might be in the possession of the Executive Branch.

On May 13, 1970, the President's response stated in part as

follows:[45]

> The power of impeachment is, of course, solely
> entrusted by the Constitution to the House of
> Representatives. However, the Executive Branch
> is clearly obligated, both by precedent and by
> the necessity of the House of Representatives hav-
> ing all of the facts before reaching its decision,
> to supply relevant information to the Legislative
> Branch, as it does in aid of other inquiries being

45/ House Committee Print, 91st Cong., 2d Sess., Associate
Justice William O. Douglas, First Report of the Special Subcommittee on H.J. Res. 920, pursuant to H. Res. 93 (1970), 13.
The President also authorized the Secretary of the Treasury to
permit inspection of certain tax returns. Id., 14. The Internal
Revenue Service made available information, including income tax
returns of Justice Douglas from 1959 to 1970, as well as returns
from organizations from which Douglas had received fees. Id., 1?
The Securities and Exchange Commission also produced information
obtained in the course of its investigation of the Parvin/Dormanr
Co., Id., 20-21. See also Brant, Impeachment, Trial and Errors
(1972), 118-121.

conducted by committees of the Congress, to the
extent compatible with the public interest.

Therefore, in accordance with the Subcommittee's
request, I shall authorize and direct appropriate
officials of the Executive Branch to furnish information within the jurisdiction of their departments and agencies relevant to the charges against
Justice Douglas and otherwise to cooperate with
the House of Representatives in this matter. As
you know, there are limitations to the President's
authority with respect to independent regulatory
agencies, but I shall express to such agencies my
desire that they cooperate to the extent permissible
by law. (Underscoring added.)

Thereafter, the Department of Justice made available to

the Special Subcommittee, through its Counsel, various papers,

documents and other material, including some in a "classified

status" and "much of it . . . raw and unevaluated," to be

used in furnishing investigative leads and not be disseminated

outside the committee or publicized in any way.[46/]

On May 22, 1973, President Nixon, speaking of the Watergate matter, stated:[47/]

Considering the number of persons involved in
this case whose testimony might be subject to a
claim of executive privilege, I recognize that a

46/ Committee Print, Associate Justice William O. Douglas,
Final Report by the Special Subcommittee on H.J. Res. 920 of the
Committee on the Judiciary, House of Representatives, 91st Cong.,
2d Sess., pursuant to H.Res. 93 (Sept. 17, 1970), 26, 28. Files
containing unevaluated data were also made available to seven
members of the House Judiciary Committee in the course of its
hearings on Congressman Gerald Ford in connection with his nom-
ination as Vice President. Washington Post, Nov. 9, 1973, A. 12.

47/ 9 Weekly Compilation of Presidential Documents, 697 (1973).

clear definition of that claim has become central
to the effort to arrive at the truth.

Accordingly, executive privilege will not be
invoked as to any testimony concerning possible
criminal conduct or discussions of possible conduct, in the matters presently under investigation,
including the Watergate affair and the alleged
cover-up.

In his State of the Union Message on January 30, 1974,

President Nixon again addressed himself to the Watergate

affair, saying: 48/

> I recognize that the House Judiciary Committee
> has a special responsibility in this area, and I
> want to indicate on this occasion that I will
> cooperate with the Judiciary Committee in its
> investigation.
>
> I will cooperate so that it can conclude its
> investigation, make its decision and I will co-
> operate in any way that I consider consistent
> with my responsibilities for the office of the
> Presidency of the United States.
>
> There is only one limitation: I will follow the
> precedent that has been followed by and defended
> by every President from George Washington to
> Lyndon B. Johnson of never doing anything that
> weakens the office of the President of the United
> States or impairs the ability of the President of
> the future to make the great decisions that are
> so essential to this Nation and the world.

48/ 10 Weekly Compilation of Presidential Documents, 121 (1974).

Department of Justice

LEGAL ASPECTS OF IMPEACHMENT: AN OVERVIEW

Appendix IV: Judicial Review of Impeachment Convictions

This appendix is a working paper prepared by the staff of the Office of Legal Counsel. The views expressed should not be regarded as an official position of the Department of Justice.

Robert G. Dixon, Jr.
Assistant Attorney General
Office of Legal Counsel

Table of Contents

Whether an impeachment conviction is subject to
judicial review

Summary

Contrary to earlier views, there is some current opinion that an impeachment conviction may be subject to judicial review. */ Raoul Berger in his Impeachment expounds the view that the framers had "no thought of delivering either the President or the Judiciary to the unbounded discretion of Congress." Under his theory, the impeachment clause must be read together with the Fifth Amendment, and if in the impeachment proceedings the limits of due process were exceeded, judicial review would lie. In view of recent decisions such as Powell v. McCormack, 395 U.S. 486 (1969), Berger feels that the "political question" doctrine would no longer be an obstacle to judicial review. John Feerick argues that the courts would have the power to declare that a particular act does not constitute a "high crime or mis-demeanor" under Article II, section 4, if/unrelated to offi- [it is a nonindictable offense] cial power. Irving Brant claims that impeachment convictions on improper grounds are in substance bills of attainder forbidden by the Constitution.

---

*/ For the purposes of our discussion here, we assume that the House of Representatives has voted the impeachment by majority vote and that the accused is an impeachable officer.

Arguments against judicial review of an impeachment conviction start with the intention of the framers to exclude the courts, and particularly the Supreme Court, from the impeachment process. The intention is evidenced by the convention debates and by early writings such as The Federalist. It also has been claimed that an impeachment does not give rise to a "case" in law or equity, as required by Article III, section 2, clause 1; and that a political question would be involved of the kind which the Supreme Court customarily has deemed nonreviewable. Concepts of the limits of the judicial function for an Article III court have been refined considerably since the Constitution was written. An attempt to enjoin the Senate proceedings, and conviction if one were entered, would produce the exact kind of clash which Chief Justice Chase decried in Mississippi v. Johnson, 4 Wall. 475, 401 (1867).

A conclusion that a presidential impeachment proceeding, and a possible conviction, were subject to judicial review would pose a serious problem for the Chief Justice should the case reach the Supreme Court. In the impeachment review, he might feel that he should recuse himself from sitting

on the ground that his role as presiding judge at the
Senate trial would create an appearance of conflict of
interest if he also sat as a member of the reviewing court.
If he did not sit, the possibility of a tie vote in the
Supreme Court would arise -- an eventuality to be avoided
at all costs. As a practical matter, it may be observed that
there is no clear statutory basis for court review of an
impeachment conviction.

None of the three recent writers favoring judicial
review discusses these critical problems of procedure and
statutory jurisdiction attendant to such review. Scholarly
comment, until recently, influenced by various considerations
just summarized, has consistently subscribed to the conclusion
that judicial review is not available in an impeachment.
This also was the view of Attorney General Kleindienst and of
former Justice Curtis in his defense of Andrew Johnson, and
Elliot Richardson has recently expressed the same view. No

Federal impeachment conviction thus far has ever been the subject of judicial review, and one Court of Claims precedent regarding impeachment of a judge holds that review would be improper.

A. Arguments in favor of judicial review

Until recently, it had been generally accepted that an impeachment conviction is final, free from any judicial review. Recent expressions of scholarly opinion--particularly those by Raoul Berger,[1] Irving Brant,[2] and John D. Feerick[3] --take a contrary view.

1. Berger's Arguments

Berger's views may be briefly summarized here.

a. His general underlying thesis is that the framers had "no thought of delivering either the President or the Judiciary to the unbounded discretion of Congress."[4] Since they regarded the judiciary as the most trustworthy branch, judicial review of impeachments may be implied in the Constitution in order to prevent arbitrary and capricious action.[5]

_____

1/ Berger, Impeachment (1973), 103-121.

2/ Brant, Impeachment, Trials and Errors (1972).

3/ Feerick, Impeaching Federal Judges: A Study of the Constitutional Provisions, 39 Fordham L. Rev. 1 (1970).

4/ Berger, op. cit. supra, at 117-118.

5/ Id., at 118-119.

b. The impeachment clauses must be read together with the Fifth Amendment providing that no person shall be deprived of "life, liberty or property without due process of law." If the Constitution does in fact limit the power of impeachment, action beyond the limit may be considered without due process of law, and such a question is properly for the courts to decide.[6]

c. The power of the Senate to try an impeachment does not authorize it to add to or change the constitutional conditions required to support a verdict of conviction. The power to try is limited by the power to convict only "on impeachment for treason, bribery or other high crimes and misdemeanors." If, as has been argued, the term "high crime and misdemeanor," as used in Article II, section 4, was intended by the framers to have the technical meaning as used in the English practice,[7] the Senate cannot declare any conduct whatsoever a "high crime or misdemeanor," and an attempt by the Senate to do so would be subject to judicial review. An analogy is Powell v. McCormack,[8] holding that in judging the qualifications of its members under Article I, section 5, clause 1, the House is limited to the qualifications prescribed in the Constitution. In the Powell case it was asserted that since the

_____

6/ Id., 120.

7/ See Appendix I regarding the meaning of "high crimes and misdemeanors."

8/ 395 U.S. 486 (1969).

-5-

Constitution vested the authority to _judge_ qualifications of Members of the Congress in each House, the Court lacked jurisdiction to review the House's decision in excluding Congressman Powell for serious misconduct. Berger's argument is that the power granted the Senate to "try" an officer in an impeachment is not substantially different than the power to "judge" the qualifications of a member of Congress. Since the Supreme Court exercised judicial review in the latter case, it could not decline review of an impeachment conviction where it is demonstrated that the Senate exceeded constitutional limits.

d. The "political question" doctrine, Berger contends, is less of an obstacle in view of decisions like _Baker_ v. _Carr_[9/] and _Powell_ v. _McCormack_.[10/] In the _Powell_ case, the Court held that the "political question" doctrine may be available only upon a showing of "a textually demonstrated constitutional commitment of the issue to a coordinate political department."[11/] Berger's argument is that at best the constitutional text here is ambiguous. While there is no express mention of judicial review in the Constitution

---

9/ 369 U.S. 186 (1962) (legislative apportionment).

10/ 395 U.S. 486 (1969) (exclusion from the House of Representatives).

11/ _Id._, at 518.

-6-

regarding impeachment, Berger maintains that the same argument could be made as to other important areas where the Constitution is equally silent as to judicial review, but where the court's authority is invoked to protect against the exercise of arbitrary governmental power.[12/]

e. Finally, although the convention debates show a clear intention to shift the function of _trying_ an impeached officer from the Court to the Senate, Berger argues that the framers' action was merely designed to shield the courts against participation in a _trial_ "crackling with political lightning," but that they do not face this danger in exercising _review_ (appellate) functions.[13/]

2. Brant's Views

Brant's view turns on his interpretation of the word "sole" as used in the impeachment clauses of Article I, section 2, clause 5, and section 3, clause 6. In his opinion, the House's "sole" power merely denies the Senate any power to impeach; the Senate's sole power merely denies the House any power to "try." There is therefore no demonstrable intention to preclude the judiciary from _review_, a concept in common parlance

---

12/ Berger, _op. cit._, _supra_, at 116-117.
13/ _Id._, at 114.

meaning _appeal_, and one entirely different from what is generally understood to be a trial. [14/]

In addition, Brant argues (as did the defenders of Andrew Johnson) that impeachment convictions on improper grounds are constitutionally proscribed bills of attainder. [15/] He maintains that an impeachment conviction which is in substance an attainder is subject to judicial review. [16/]

3. Feerick's Views

Feerick's view is that any extension of impeachment to nonindictable offenses not connected with the use of official power was not intended by the framers and finds no support in English impeachment precedents. [17/] In his opinion, the Supreme Court has, "as in the case of other legislative acts, the power to declare that a particular act does not constitute a 'high Crime and Misdemeanor' and, therefore, that Congress exceeded its power in removing an official." [18/]

14/ Brant, at 183. On the other hand, Brant points out that Benjamin R. Curtis, a former Justice of the Supreme Court, and one of Johnson's attorneys, acknowledged "the absence of review." _Id._, at 186-187.

15/ _Id._, at 133-54, 181-200.

16/ _Id._, at 182-193.

17/ Feerick, _supra_, 39 Fordham L. Rev. at 54-55 (1970); see also Daugherty, Limitations upon Impeachment, 23 Yale L.J. 60, 70-71 (1913).

18/ Feerick, _supra_ at 57.

-8-

B. Arguments against Judicial Review

The arguments against judicial review are based on (1) the intention of the framers, (2) specific jurisdictional provisions of the Constitution which restrict the courts to acting in a "case or controversy" under Article III, and the self-imposed restraint against a review of "political questions," (3) lack of precedent, and (4) the weight of scholarly authority.

1. The Intention of the Framers

It can be argued that the framers considered and rejected giving the courts any role in the impeachment process. If, as the framers thought, the courts should not be drawn into a political controversy involving impeachment of the President either in the impeaching or trial stage, it is most unlikely that they would have intended to confer ultimate authority on the courts to review such proceedings and undo the results of an impeachment conviction.

Turning to the Convention, the first drafts of the Constitution submitted to the framers provided that the jurisdiction of the national judiciary should extend to impeachments of national officers--impeachment by the inferior courts, and trial by the Supreme Court.[19/] Subsequently, this provision

---

19/ Appendix II describes in detail the deliberations in the Convention which finally resulted in exclusion of the courts from impeachment proceedings.

-9-

was deleted and the power to impeach was conferred on the House of Representatives.[20/]   Next, an attempt was made to give the Supreme Court original jurisdiction "in cases of impeachment."[21/]   This was rejected and the decision was that impeachments be tried by the Senate.[22/]

The Senate was selected as the proper impeachment tribunal, notwithstanding protests that legislative control over impeachment made the executive too dependent upon the legislature.[23/]   However, to avoid even greater dependence, the Convention did provide for a President to be elected independently of the legislature.[24/]   Thus, the determination to make the Senate the impeachment tribunal was largely a political compromise between two groups of Convention delegates, those who favored and those who opposed a high degree of executive independence from the legislature.   It was recognized by Wilson, who opposed making the Senate the impeachment tribunal, that

---

20/   2 Farrand, Records of the Federal Convention of 1787 (rev. ed. 1966) (hereafter "Farrand"), 186.

21/   Id.; Foster, Constitution of the United States (1895), § 88.

22/   2 Farrand 493; Foster, op. cit. supra, § 89.

23/   See, e.g. 2 Farrand 66.

24/   See, e.g. 2 Farrand 103-105, 109-111.

the Senate's impeachment power blended legislative and judicial power in one branch of government.[25/] The Convention nevertheless determined to give the Senate the "sole" power to try impeachments.

Because the Senate's power to try impeachments was established as a legislative check upon the executive, and recognized as a departure from normal separation of powers principles, an inference can be drawn that the federal judiciary was to have no power to review a Senate conviction in an impeachment. Morris indicated that abuse of the Senate's power to try impeachments would be self-contained because that body would not "say untruly on their oaths that the President was guilty of crimes or facts, especially as in four years he can be turned out."[26/] If judicial review in such cases had been intended, it may be questioned whether some of the Convention delegates would have contended so vigorously that the impeachment provisions made the executive too dependent on the legislature. Moreover, no statement during the Convention suggested that judicial review was intended in cases of impeachment.

25/   2 Farrand 522-523.

26/   2 Farrand 551.

Available records concerning state ratification conventions also suggest that judicial review of impeachment was not contemplated.[27] During debates at state conventions, various checks upon the impeachment power were mentioned (e.g., the two-stage process, the role of the Chief Justice as presiding officer when a President is being tried, the fact that members of Congress are accountable to the electorate), but there appears to be no record of any statement to the effect that judicial review of impeachment convictions would be available.

---

[27] A more detailed discussion of the state ratification conventions is contained in Appendix II.

The historical reasons against judicial involvement in impeachments are comprehensively discussed by Story[29], who draws heavily on Hamilton's _Federalist_ paper on the subject[30]. The reasons which they assigned may briefly be noted:

a. Impeachments are of a nature described as "political", since they relate to injuries done to the public itself. Their prosecution will seldom fail to agitate the passions of the Nation, dividing it into parties, those friendly and those hostile to the accused. The Convention thought that the Senate was the fittest body to deal with a matter so deeply affecting the person whose political reputation was at stake. There was precedent in Great Britain for this procedure, since it was the province of the House of Commons to prefer the impeachment, and the House of Lords to decide it.

---

[29] Story, Commentaries on the Constitution of the United States (1970 Ed.), Vol. II, 227-245. Warren, The Making of the Constitution (1928), 658-664; see also petitioner's brief in Richard M. Nixon v. President etc. v. Sirica, on appeal (D.C. App. No. 73-1962), 9 Weekly Compilation of Presidential Documents, 1101, 1105-1106 (Sept. 17, 1973).

[30] The Federalist, No. 65 (J.E. Cooke Ed.), 439-445.

Several of the State constitutions had already followed that example.$^{31/}$

b. The Supreme Court, it was _then_ felt, could not be relied on as well as the Senate to perform this task for several reasons. The framers preferred a larger body such as the Senate, since the "awful discretion" involved in a court of impeachment, "to doom to honor or to infamy the most confidential and the most distinguished characters of the community, forbids the commitment of the trust to a small number of persons." $^{32/}$ In the Senate, the matter would never be tied down by "strict rules, either in the delineation of the offense by the prosecutors or in the construction of it . . . ." $^{33/}$

31/ In all the States the lower branch was empowered to impeach. There was less uniformity among the States as to the trial. In Virginia and Maryland the trial was by the courts; in New York and South Carolina by a special court consisting of the Senate and the judges; in the other States, the upper branch of the legislature tried impeachments. Warren, The Making of the Constitution (1928), 659. See Appendix II.

32/ The Federalist, op. cit. supra, at 441-442.

33/ Id., 441.

c. Another reason given by Hamilton and Story for selecting the Senate rather than the Supreme Court was that the Court might later be called on to review criminal proceedings, and it would have been unjust to place in the same hands both the impeachment decision and the outcome of the subsequent criminal proceeding.[34/] Moreover, if the Court were made up chiefly of the President's appointees, any decision in his favor would be suspect.

d. Other considerations were that to place such power in the Judicial branch would serve as "pretexts for clamour" against that process, and possibly damage the Court's reputation.

[34/] A related problem involved in judicial review is the role that the Chief Justice plays as presiding officer at a Presidential impeachment trial, where he is called on to rule on the admissibility or exclusion of certain evidence. In the Johnson trial, his rulings were subject to being overturned by the Senate. On review of an impeachment conviction, it might be argued that Senate rulings reversing the Chief Judge could be viewed as depriving the accused of a fair trial. Moreover, if the matter reached the Supreme Court, the Chief Justice would be in the difficult position of having either to disqualify himself or to pass upon the correctness of his own prior rulings. The fact that the Supreme Court is called on at times to pass upon both a civil and a criminal case with somewhat similar issues and the same defendant is not quite an apt parallel.

While judicial tenure of office during good behavior was recognized as desirable for the independent discharge of customary judicial functions, such a tenure made it undesirable for judges to deal with impeachable offenses--the decision of which should be made by a body such as the Senate that could more directly be held responsible by the people through the elective process.

2. Jurisdictional Objections.

One of the possible jurisdictional objections to review of impeachment convictions by the courts was advanced by House Manager John A. Bingham during the Senate trial of Andrew Johnson, namely that an impeachment would not give rise to a "case" in law or equity, as required by Article III, sec. 2, cl. 1.[35/]

A related argument was that impeachment involved a political question, which courts have generally refrained from considering.[36/] Cases such as Baker v. Carr and

---

[35/] Brant asserts that this argument is lacking in merit. He claims that when an ousted officer appeals his conviction, or sues for his salary, or brings an action for quo warranto to contest his successor's right to office, the litigation constitutes a "case" with requisite substantiality, adversity and ripeness. Brant, op. cit. supra, 184-185.

[36/] See Scharpf, Judicial Review and the Political Question: A Functional Analysis, 75 Yale L.J. 517, 539 (1966); The Supreme Court, 1968 Term, 83 Harv. L. Rev. 7, 62-72 (1969).

Powell v. McCormack, reflecting a trend toward judicial review of "political" type questions, can be distinguished upon the ground that there was absent in those cases the specific intent manifested in the Convention of closing the door to any judicial role in impeachment proceedings. In addition, the Baker line of cases was bottomed on a concept of personal voting right protectible under the Fourteenth Amendment, and Powell was bottomed on a simplistic view of three precise self-defining requirements for House eligibility. Impeachment is different. No "voting" or "civil" right is involved; and there is no precision in the constitutional definition of impeachable offenses.

  3. Lack of Precedent.

    Thus far, no aspect of a federal impeachment or impeachment conviction has been the direct subject of judicial review. In Mississippi v. Johnson,[37] reference was made to the hypothetical case of the House of Representatives having impeached the President and an injunction being sought to restrain the Senate from sitting as a court of impeachment.

----

[37] 4 Wall 475 (1867).

Speaking for the Court, Chief Justice Chase stated (by way

of dictum):[38/]

> "Would the strange spectacle be offered to the
> public world of an attempt by this Court to
> arrest proceedings in that (Senate) court?
>
> These questions answer themselves."

After Judge Halsted L. Ritter was impeached, he sued

for his salary in the Court of Claims, claiming that the

Senate had exceeded its jurisdiction in trying him on charges

that did not constitute impeachable offenses under the Consti-

tution. The Court disclaimed jurisdiction on the ground that

the Senate's jurisdiction and power were exclusive. Citing

Mississippi v. Johnson, supra, the Court of Claims stated

that the power of impeachment vested in the Senate and the

House was essentially "political" and not subject to judicial

review.[39/] After reviewing the relevant Convention history

and scholarly opinion, the Court said:[40/]

> While the Senate in one sense acts as a court
> on the trial of an impeachment, it is essentially

[38/]Id. at 501.

[39/]Ritter v. United States, 84 Ct. Cls. 293, 300 (1936), cert.
denied, 300 U.S. 668 (1937).

[40/]84 C. Cls. at 299. In the Brief for the United States in
Opposition to Certiorari, Solicitor General Reed stated that
the decision of the Court of Claims that it had no jurisdiction
to look behind the impeachment judgment was "clearly correct."
Relying on the terms and history of the Constitution the
Solicitor General maintained that "impeachment proceedings are
committed exclusively to Congress."

- 18 -

a political body and in its actions is influenced
by the views of its members on the public welfare.
The courts, on the other hand, are expected to
render their decisions according to the law regard-
less of the consequences. This must have been
realized by the members of the Constitutional
Convention and in rejecting proposals to have impeachments tried by a court composed of regularly
appointed judges we think it avoided the possibility of unseemly conflicts between a political
body such as the Senate and the judicial tribunals
which might determine the case on different principles.

4. Scholarly Opinion.

The leading exponents of the position that there is

a right of judicial review over impeachments are, as noted,

Berger, Brant and Ferrick. Although more current, theirs is

probably the minority view. These writers make no claim

that there is such a right in every case, but primarily where

in fact "no high crime or misdemeanor" was committed, or due

process or other constitutional rights had been denied. We

are not aware of any judicial holding that a federal impeach-

ment conviction can be set aside upon these or other grounds,

nor do such objections appear to have affected the contrary

conclusions reached by earlier scholars.

Some representative expressions of the majority view may

be cited.

Willoughby says:[41/]

> It is scarcely necessary to say that the proceed-
> ing and determinations of the Senate when sitting
> as a court of impeachment are not subject to review
> in any other court.

Black says:[42/]

> It will be perceived that the power to determine
> what crimes are impeachable rests very much with
> congress. For the house, before preferring
> articles of impeachment, will decide whether the
> acts or conduct complained of constitute a "high
> crime or misdemeanor." And the senate, in trying
> the case, will also have to consider the same
> question. If, in the judgment of the senate, the
> offense charged is not impeachable, they will
> acquit; otherwise upon sufficient proof and the
> concurrence of the necessary majority, they will
> convict. And in either case, there is no other
> power which can review or reverse their decision.
> (Underscoring added.)

In accord are many other writers on the subject.[43/] A

contemporary opinion is expressed by Professor Herbert Wechsler

as follows: [44/]

[41/]3 Willoughby, The Constitutional Law of the United States
(2d Ed.), 1451.

[42/]Black, Constitutional Law (1895), pp. 121-122.

[43/]See e.g., Dwight, Trial by Impeachment, 15 Amer. L.Reg. 257,
258 (1866): Story, Commentaries of the Constitution of the
United States (1970 Ed.), Vol. II, 277, who says the judgment,
when once pronounced becomes "absolute and irreversible."
Thomas, The Law of Impeachment in the United States, 2 Am.Pol.
Sci.Rev. 378, 393 (1908), "From their decision there is no appeal."

[44/]Wechsler, Toward Neutral Principles of Constitutional Law,
73 Harv. L.Rev. 1, 8 (1959). Berger points out that Wechsler's
assertion in the same article that the "seating" of a Representative is also not subject to judicial review ha now been
repudiated by the Supreme Court in Powell v. McCormack, supra.
Berger, op. cit. supra, at 104.

Who, for example, would contend that the civil courts may properly review a judgment of impeachment when article I, section 3 declares that the "sole Power to try" is in the Senate? That any proper trial of an impeachment may present issues of the most important constitutional dimension, as Senator Kennedy reminds us in his moving story of the Senator whose vote saved Andrew Johnson, is simply immaterial in this connection.

So also, former Attorney General Kleindienst maintained that once the President is impeached by the Senate "there is no court of appeal."[45/] A discussion of the matter of judicial review is contained in the 1974 report, "The Law of Presidential Impeachment" prepared by the Committee of Federal Legislation of the Association of the City of New York. The committee concludes that the federal judiciary

---

45/ Executive privilege, etc., Hearings before the Subcommittee on Intergovernmental Relations of the Committee on Government Operations and the Subcommittees on Separation of Powers and Administrative Practice and Procedure of the Committee on the Judiciary, U.S. Senate, 93d Cong. 1st Sess., on S. 1142, etc. (1973), 45. Moreover, Benjamin R. Curtis, one of the attorneys for Andrew Johnson, conceded that when the Senate sits in the "special trial" of an impeachment, the proceedings are "incapable of review." Brant, op. cit. supra, at 137.

lacks authority to review impeachment judgments of removal

for errors either of procedure or substance.[46/]

46/ Report, The Law of Presidential Impeachment, Jan. 21, 1974, pp. 14-17. Most recently, the contrary view on this subject was stated by Professor Eugene V. Rostow, former Dean of the Yale Law School, as follows:

> The debate over the constitutional scope of impeachment is not a question to be resolved only by Congress, by public opinion or by political means. The courts may well step in, as the umpire of the Constitution, and insist that impeachment proceedings be brought only on one or more of the grounds specified in the Constitution. ("The Question of Impeachment," Washington Post, February 3, 1974, C 2).

CPSIA information can be obtained
at www.ICGtesting.com
Printed in the USA
BVHW011434130819
555664BV00018BA/1388/P